Sexual
McCarthyism

Sexual McCarthyism

Clinton,
Starr, and the
Emerging Constitutional Crisis

ALAN M. DERSHOWITZ

BASIC BOOKS

A Member of the Perseus Books Group

To my mother Claire,
who always tells me not to argue so much.

Published by Basic Books,
A Member of the Perseus Books Group.

FIRST EDITION

Designed by Elliott Beard

C.I.P. data has been applied for.

ISBN 0-465-01628-6

Contents

The Investigation Begins: Whitewater

CHAPTER IV
Monica Lewinsky:
Is It About Sex or About Lying About Sex?

CHAPTER V

The Constitutional Crisis:
Impeachment, Resignation, Censure?

Acknowledgments

I could not possibly have produced this book without the enormous assistance of John Orsini, who in addition to doing much of the research and organizing of the columns and chronology, also counseled and guided me throughout the process. Gina Petrocelli and Hanna Liebman assisted me in compiling the columns for my class materials. My thanks also to Devany Vallencourt who typed much of the manuscript.

Many callers and letter-writers encouraged me to write this book. The idea for it first occurred over a dinner conversation with the writer Philip Roth to whom I used the term "sexual McCarthyism." He urged me to write something about that concept and I thank him for his encouragement while taking full responsibility for its implementation. My agents Helen Rees and David Hendin made this possible along with Don Fehr at Basic Books and his wonderful editorial staff.

My usual thanks to my wonderful family who always tells it as it is. Special appreciation to my daughter Ella whose constant question over the past months has been: "Do we have to talk about President Clinton again?" And thanks to the students in the class I am currently teaching about the presidential investigation for always asking the right questions.

Sexual
McCarthyism

How Did We Get Here?

The greatest constitutional crisis in modern American history may turn on whether the President of the United States told a sex lie under oath and tried—unsuccessfully—to keep secret an improper sexual relationship. The titillating background to this crisis has obscured the profound issues of state that may be involved in the upcoming confrontation among the Presidency, the Judiciary, the Congress, and this strange anomaly called the Independent Counsel.

As a teacher and practitioner of law, I have been profoundly interested in this conflict from the very beginning. I have written about every phase of the case from the initial appointment of an Independent Counsel, to the Paula Jones lawsuit, to the decision to give Monica Lewinsky immunity, to the President's testimony, to the release of the Independent Counsel's referral, to the move toward initiating impeachment proceedings. I have also been teaching about the constitutional, ethical, criminal, tactical and strategic issues raised in this case in my classes at Harvard Law School. In my writings and teaching I have addressed the broader issues of enduring concern that transcend current events. These issues include:

Why the independent counsel law is a necessary evil, but why the appointment of Kenneth Starr was improper.

Why the President's private life is the business of the American public—to a degree.

Why the Supreme Court was right in requiring the President to submit to the Paula Jones lawsuit.

Why the President and his lawyers were wrong in not settling or defaulting that lawsuit rather than submitting to a deposition about the President's sex life.

Why Starr's leaking of testimony and evidence are at least as serious obstructions of justice as anything alleged against the President.

Why it is dangerous to allow an Independent Counsel to probe the sex lives of public officials.

Why a sitting President cannot be indicted and tried unless he is *first* impeached.

Whether President Clinton committed perjury or obstruction of justice—and does it matter?

What constitutional rights does a President have when he is the target of a grand jury or impeachment process?

What is the legal status of the referral by the Independent Counsel, and why is this report so dangerous?

What are the constitutional criteria for removing a President, and why they are different for judges, Senators and CEOs?

What would an impeachment and removal trial look like?

How the President can still survive and complete his term.

What the lasting constitutional, historical and political legacies of this case are likely to be.

I have also written about the President's record on civil liberties and the contrast between his demand for privacy and due process for himself and his apparent lack of concern for privacy and due process for others.

By bringing these essays (and several relevant earlier columns) together, and by introducing them with this overview, I hope to answer many of the questions that are currently being asked by Americans and raise some that are not being adequately discussed. I am neither an uncritical Clinton partisan—though I oppose his impeachment—nor an uncritical Starr partisan. I have criticized both sides and raised questions that are disturbing to each.

At the beginning of the investigation I was supportive of the appointment of an Independent Counsel to investigate Whitewater, Filegate and the Travel Office. I also supported the continuation of the Paula Jones lawsuit (see Chapters I and III). I began to worry when Kenneth Starr replaced Robert Fiske as Independent Counsel (see Chapter II). My concern grew when Starr managed to persuade both Janet Reno and the court to expand his jurisdiction into the Monica Lewinsky matter (see Chapter IV). Though the justification put forward for expanding the investigation dealt with buying the silence of witnesses, I immediately suspected that the Hubbell-Jordan connection was merely a pretext for what I began to call "sexual McCarthyism"—a term that has now been used widely to characterize the danger of Starr's inquisition into Clinton's sex life. There is a compelling analogy to what Senator McCarthy, Roy Cohn and J. Edgar Hoover did back in the 1950s: they investigated the private sexual behavior of public figures in order to influence their public actions (see Chapter IV).

At bottom this is a story of how two men who are obsessed about forbidden sex—Clinton about engaging in it and Starr about exposing it—managed to turn a tawdry series of Oval Office sexual encounters into a constitutional crisis. Clinton and his advisers made mistake after mistake in a futile effort to keep his embarrassing little secret from becoming public. Starr and his staff overreached, overreacted, exaggerated and pressed every issue to the limits of its logic to expose the secret and embarrass the President. The result was a highly unlikely combination of factors that led the nation to where almost no one (except the extreme right) wanted to go—to the brink of a constitutional crisis with international implications.

It is also a story about lawyers and their unprecedented influence on matters of governance. The two alleged crimes that are at the core of what Starr believes are impeachable offenses were committed by Clinton (a lawyer) in the presence of his lawyers and are based on answers he gave to questions asked by other lawyers. Now lawyers are debating the legal niceties of whether the President's statements constitute the highly technical crime of perjury—as well as whether they are impeachable offenses under the Constitution. Many Americans, both in and out of Congress, are outraged at the legalisms employed by the President and his lawyers. They ask, "Why can't the President just admit he lied?" The answer inheres in the nature of the legal and constitutional system under which we live. The virtue of the rule of law (over the fiat of man and woman) is that it is—at least in theory—predictable because it is written down in precise language that gives fair warning to all. The vice of the rule of law is that precise language encourages precisely the kind of hairsplitting legalisms that so many deplore. In this book, I try to explain why laws and lawyers have become so central to our lives, and how to strike an appropriate balance between the rule of law and the tyranny of technicality.

But first we must understand how we got to where we are. I begin with the remarkable series of blunders committed by President Clinton and his advisers.

How We Got to Where We Are

Doctors conduct autopsies on patients who die, business schools do post-mortems on companies that failed, coaches watch videos of games in which they were beaten, and lawyers analyze cases they lost. The purpose is to learn from mistakes. As Santayana said: "Those who cannot remember the past are condemned to repeat it."

It is in the spirit of Santayana that I look back at the history of mistakes, misjudgments, blunders and lost opportunities that led President Clinton to the uncomfortable place he now finds himself. It does not take a Monday morning quarterback to identify the worst of the errors. They were obvious at the time to any discerning eye. Indeed, the President was warned in advance about virtually every one of them, and he chose to ignore the warnings and listen to those who called for short-term solutions—quick fixes—to what became long-term problems.

In my thirty-five years of practicing and teaching law, I have seen this pattern repeated by people who eventually get into trouble. They mortgage their future to obtain immediate gratification—political, economic or sexual. They believe that when the future finally arrives, there will be new quick fixes. And usually they are right. It generally requires a combination of unlikely factors to produce disaster, and most successful people are good at reducing risks. But even the most successful people are subject to probabilities, and eventually—if they persist in their reckless behavior—the statistics will catch up with them. It is important, therefore, to examine the White House's pattern of preferring short-term tactical fixes over long-term strategic solutions that led to the current crisis.

There were a handful of crucial decision points along the road to disaster. At every point, the President and his advisers opted for the short-term political tactic that helped them get good headlines and poll results, rather than the longer term strategy which might have prevented an entirely lawful sexual indiscretion from turning into a possible crime.

Clinton's Initial Decision: Sex with Lewinsky

The first—and most important—point was the President's foolhardy decision to engage in a surreptitious sexual relationship with a White House intern at a time when he knew he was under intense investigation by a puritanical prosecutor, and was subject to a lawsuit for sexual harassment by a vindictive woman who was represented by politically motivated lawyers.

If there was indeed a "right-wing conspiracy" out there waiting to "get" the President, it is difficult to imagine any action more reckless than Oval Office sex with a young blabbermouth whose goal was probably as much to brag about her conquest of the President as to engage in an intimate relationship. She really did want oral sex: she wanted to talk about it. And she did—to more than a dozen people. The President achieved immediate gratification while risking long-term consequences to his marriage, his daughter, his presidency and above all the nation's stability. At the time he began his sexual encounter with Lewinsky, Clinton knew that he might possibly have to testify under oath about his sex life. He knew that two sets of enemies had the powerful legal weapon of subpoena power aimed directly at his heart. That is probably why he was reluctant to engage in sexual intercourse—or, initially, even completed oral sex. He wanted sex with deniability. What he got was unsatisfying sex with unconvincing deniability. Or, as Maureen Dowd put it: "Mr. Clinton's habit with language and behavior has been to try to incorporate his alibi into his sin. The result is more twisted than titillating."[1]

This was surely not the first time Bill Clinton put his future at risk for immediate sexual gratification. But in every other instance he was able to avoid the long-term consequences. I am certain that he believed that this pattern of short-term risk-taking and subsequent avoidance of long-term consequences would be repeated. I doubt he believed, at the moment that he first allowed Lewinsky to touch him in a sexual manner, that this action would eventually lead to possible removal from office and damage to his family life. He surely would not have consciously taken such a knowing risk. But when people have succeeded so often in the past in achieving both immediate gratification and long-term avoidance of consequences, they miscalculate the odds and act as if they can have their cake and eat it too.

The history of many of my own clients over three decades is largely a history of defendants who for years—sometimes decades—have risked their careers, family lives, fortunes and freedom for some form of immediate gratification. Finally when they were caught, everyone asked the same question: "How could they have risked so much for so little?" What that question fails to understand is that the "little" thing for which they were eventually caught was usually only the tip of a very large iceberg of sin or crime that they had gotten away with for years. In their minds, therefore, they were risking very little (the extreme unlikelihood that this time they would get caught) for a great deal (a lifetime of small, short term gratifications, which add up to something for which it is worth taking small risks).

In retrospect, we consider such actions reckless because we are running the video backwards: we know he was caught. But at the time Clinton made the decision, he probably did not regard it as any more reckless than the many similar decisions he had previously made, without destroying his career and his family. He had probably played the same sexual-verbal game before: limiting his sexual contact so that he could plausibly deny that he engaged in "sexual relationships" outside of his marriage,[2] but he never before had to testify under oath about these relationships. What he failed to comprehend was how much the risks had increased as the result of the legal proceedings then in place—the Jones lawsuit and the Starr investigation. These legal proceedings escalated the stakes by turning a private sexual encounter into the subject of sworn testimony and investigation by an independent counsel. But it could have remained merely an improper sexual relationship had Clinton made the correct decisions before he denied under oath that he had engaged in sexual relations with Lewinsky.

The Appointment of an Independent Counsel

Before we can fully evaluate President Clinton's disastrous decision to testify at the Jones deposition and later at the Starr grand jury, it is important to look back at the appointment of Kenneth Starr as the Independent Counsel and Clinton's response to that appointment.

The entire concept of an independent counsel is an anomaly made necessary by a structural defect in our system of government. Every other civilized nation in the world seeks to depoliticize the investigative and prosecutorial decisions. They have a permanent office of prosecution outside the political system. Generally there are two entirely separate offices and officers that comprise what we lump together as the Department of Justice and the Attorney General.

Our Attorney General is a presidential appointee, generally from the President's party, often a trusted friend and political adviser. Recall Robert Kennedy, President Kennedy's brother and campaign manager: John Mitchell, President Nixon's law partner and campaign manager; and William French-Smith,

President Reagan's personal lawyer, as perhaps the most striking examples of the closeness between Presidents and their Attorneys General. Although Janet Reno was not a friend of Bill Clinton, she came from his party and was recommended for the job by Hillary Rodham Clinton's brother. The Attorney General is supposed to be a trusted loyalist, a member of the President's Cabinet, a person in whom the President can confide on matters of policy and politics. That same Attorney General is also suppose to be the nation's highest law enforcement officer—the person who ultimately decides whom to investigate and to prosecute.

Because our Attorney General—unlike any official in other governments—plays these dual roles of political adviser and chief prosecutor, no one holding that job can be trusted to investigate and, if necessary, prosecute the President or other higher-ranking members of his or her and the Attorney General's administration. He or she would be in a clear conflict of interest, and the perception of unfairness would cloud any decision.

In all other democracies, the two jobs that our Attorney General perform are divided. There is a political office generally called the "Minister of Justice" whose job it is to advise the president or prime minister and to be loyal to the party and person in power; there is also a non-political official, generally called the "Attorney General" or the "Director of Public Prosecutors," who has no loyalty to the incumbent head of state or his party and whose sole responsibility is to investigate and prosecute in a nonpartisan manner. Prime ministers and presidents have been brought down (and upheld) by such prosecutors, without any appearance of impropriety.

Our system of investigation and prosecution is unique in the world. We have politicized the role of prosecutor, not only at the federal level but in all of our states and counties as well. Nowhere else are prosecutors (or judges) elected. Indeed, it is unthinkable in most parts of the world to have prosecutors run for office, make campaign promises and solicit contributions. Prosecutors in other countries are civil servants who do not pander to the people's understandable wish to be safe from crime, or campaign on the promise to "be tough on crime." (Our penchant for voting on everything has reached laughable proportions in Florida, where even "public defenders" must run for office. I can only imagine what the campaign must be like.) But in the United States, prosecutors are not only elected, but the job is a stepping stone to higher office, as evidenced by the fact that nearly every Senator or Congressman who ever practiced law once served as a prosecutor. Even President Clinton began his political career as the elected Attorney General of Arkansas.

Because our system of prosecution has become so politicized and because the role of Attorney General of the United States merges the political with the prosecutorial, it has become necessary to create the Office of Independent Counsel. When evidence of improprieties surrounding Whitewater began to emerge, it became evident that an independent counsel would have to be appointed.

Because the Independent Counsel Law—which vests the selection in a panel of judges—had lapsed, Attorney General Janet Reno at first decided that she would have to appoint a special prosecutor to investigate President Clinton. She appointed a moderate Republican named Robert Fiske, who had long experience as both a federal prosecutor and a private lawyer. But Republican Senators conspired with a Republican judge to remove Fiske and have Kenneth Starr appointed (see Chapter II). Although Starr's reputation as a right-wing ideologue and ambitious Republican politician were well known, White House Counsel Abner Mikva—who had served as an appellate judge alongside Starr—assured President Clinton that Starr would be fair. The White House accepted the appointment without challenge, although there were obvious problems with the manner in which the appointment was made, and clear conflicts of interest in the appointee. Starr was appointed following a lunch meeting between one of the appointing judges and two right-wing Senators from tobacco states, and Starr was representing cigarette producers who were eager to see an end to the Clinton presidency. It was later learned that Starr had given legal advice to Jones's lawyers prior to his appointment to Independent Counsel. The stage was thus set for a clash between two men who shared different obsessions about the same subject—forbidden sex. But before any of the President's private sexual activities could become the subject of Starr's prosecutorial agenda, the President had to give Starr one of the greatest gifts anyone can give an overzealous prosecutor—a deposition under oath about his private sex life.

The Decision to Testify at the Jones Deposition

It is unlikely that Bill Clinton confided the truth of his relationship with Monica Lewinsky to any of his lawyers. He couldn't, because David Kendall was representing both him and his wife. Robert Bennett, though representing only President Clinton, was sharing information with Kendall. Thus if President Clinton did not want his wife to find out about Lewinsky, he could not tell either Bennett or Kendall. It is likely that his lawyers (and his wife) suspected the possibility that there was some truth to the rumors that something untoward had occurred between Bill Clinton and Monica Lewinsky. After all, Clinton did tell his lawyers—and did testify—that he engaged in adulterous sex with Gennifer Flowers, despite his previous public denial. Moreover, his reputation as a "womanizer" was well known. Any lawyer worth his salt should have based decisions regarding the President's testimony on the assumption that he may well have engaged in a sexual relationship with Monica Lewinsky, despite any assurances to the contrary. A good lawyer should also have assumed that a twenty-two-year-old intern who had engaged in a sexual relationship with the President of the United States would talk about it.

Robert Bennett was on notice that the President was going to be asked about Lewinsky. If he conducted any kind of investigation to determine the nature of their relationship, he would surely have uncovered the widespread concern around the White House over Monica Lewinsky's unusual access to the President. He would also have learned of the dozens of logged meetings between the President and a young government employee. This should have put Bennett on notice to probe more deeply. At the very least he should have interviewed Lewinsky, confronted her with the concerns, and asked her direct questions. He should also have interviewed those White House officials who had expressed concern. Yet, on the basis of little more than an assurance from the President, he allowed an affidavit to be submitted by Lewinsky denying any sexual relationship. Putting aside the ethical issues arising from relying on an affidavit that he was on notice might well be false, and having his client testify to facts that he had to suspect might be false, it is difficult to understand the tactical considerations that led the President's lawyers to allow him to testify about his sex life.

It is not as if Bennett had not been cautioned about the risks of having the President testify about his sex life at the Jones deposition. On May 27, 1997, six months before President Clinton testified at a deposition in the Paula Jones lawsuit, I made the following remarks on the Geraldo Rivera Show:

> This case never should have gotten this far. It should have been settled early when he could have settled it easily. He must settle the case . . .
>
> Remember, depositions are very broad in latitude. He could be asked questions about adultery. He could be asked questions about his prior sexual life. There are no relevancy objections that are generally sustained to depositions . . .
>
> I think the President could win if it actually went to trial, but it won't go to trial. What I would do if I were his lawyer is to say, "Look, the dignity of the office precludes the President from answering any of these questions. We realize that as a result of not answering these questions, we will reluctantly, without admitting anything, have to be sanctioned by having the verdict directed against us on the merits. We accept that, because we can't answer the questions and preserve the dignity. And now let's move on to the damages, where the focus is not on the President but on Paula Jones."

And in that way, he can, in effect, settle the case, even if the other side doesn't settle because the damages will be very low, there won't be an apology. There'll be a judgment against him, but the judgment will be explained on the basis of the dignity of the presidency. So if the settlement talks fail, that's what I would recommend that his lawyers think about . . .

And the President has to start asking himself: Is he well advised here?

The President had three options, but he was aware of only two of them. He knew that he could litigate and try to win— as he ended up doing. He also knew that he could try to settle the case, which would have avoided the necessity of testifying at the deposition or trial. A settlement requires both sides to agree. In the Jones case, the President reportedly offered to pay Jones $700,000, in order to settle the case. Jones insisted on an apology[3] and the settlement talks eventually broke down.

The third option, of which the President was unaware, was to default the Jones case. Every litigant in a civil case has the right to default—which means, essentially, to settle the case unilaterally by simply refusing to contest the allegations in the complaint. Consider, for example, the following hypothetical: a fired employee of a high-tech business sues for $10,000 in back pay. The business realizes that in order to defend its actions, it would have to reveal commercial secrets valued at $1,000,000 and take the time of executives that it estimates at being worth $200,000. It offers to settle the case for the $10,000 that the employee is demanding, but the angry employee prefers a trial at which he will be publicly vindicated. The company has the right simply to default, have the judgment entered against it, and have the court order it to pay the damages sought by the employee. No stigma is attached to defaulting a case. It does not even necessarily entail an admission of liability. It represents a practical assessment of the costs and benefits of litigating and not litigating—just as a settlement does.

Robert Bennett never told President Clinton that he could have defaulted and paid Jones far less than the $700,000 he offered without making any apology. Nor did he tell the President that he could have used the threat of defaulting to increase the chances of securing a settlement. Bennett could have approached the Jones lawyers and told them that under no circumstances would there be a trial: the only options were default or settlement. A default would probably result in monetary judgment of less than $100,000—damages in such cases tend to be in the range of $25,000 to $50,000. Moreover, there would be no apology of any kind. To the contrary, the President would assert his absolute innocence and release a statement explaining why he had no choice but to default, since litigation would take too much valuable time from his presidential duties. Settlement, on the other hand, would result in a payment of $700,000. Faced with these options, it is likely that the Jones lawyers would have accepted a settlement and Clinton would never have had to testify about his sex life in any proceedings. Perhaps the Lewinsky story would have leaked, but the President would not have had to dignify a rumor with a response. It was the entirely avoidable decision to have him testify under oath—not once, but twice—that turned a sex rumor into a possibly impeachable offense.

How do I know that Robert Bennett never told President Clinton of the default option? Because both men personally told me. Here is the story, being told publicly for the first time.

On January 17, 1998, President Clinton was deposed in the Paula Jones lawsuit and was asked questions about his relationship with Monica Lewinsky. Among the questions were the following:

Did you have an extramarital sexual affair with Monica Lewinsky?

If she told someone that she had a sexual affair with you beginning in November of 1995, would that be a lie?

I think I used the term "sexual affair." And so the record is completely clear, have you ever had sexual relations with Monica Lewinsky, as that term is defined in Deposition Exhibit 1, as modified by the Court?

Clinton answered as follows:

I have never had sexual relations with Monica Lewinsky. I've never had an affair with her.

His answer was based on the following definition of sexual relations accepted by the judge:

For the purpose of this deposition, a person engages in "sexual relations" when the person knowingly engages in or causes

1. contact with the genitalia, anus, groin, breast, inner thigh, or buttocks of any person with an intent to arouse or gratify the sexual desire of any person;

"Contact" means intentional touching, either directly or through clothing.

After the Jones lawyers completed their questioning, the President's own lawyer, Robert Bennett, asked the following question:

In paragraph eight of her affidavit, [Monica Lewinsky] says this, "I have never had a sexual relationship with the president, he did not propose that we have a sexual relationship, he did not offer employment or other benefits in exchange for a sexual relationship, he did not deny me employment or other benefits for rejecting a sexual relationship."

Is that a true and accurate statement?

The President responded: "That is absolutely true."

Shortly thereafter, reports began to appear of tape-recorded conversations between Linda Tripp and Monica Lewinsky suggesting that there had been a sexual relationship of some kind between the President and Monica Lewinsky.

On January 23, 1998, I appeared on the MSNBC program

"Internight" and criticized Bennett for allowing the President to walk into a perjury trap and a swearing contest. I recommended that the President "get out in front of this story. He has to tell the truth, and if the truth is inculpatory he has to tell it." I recommended that the President "get a new lawyer, tell him the truth, sit down with your new lawyer . . . and [have him give you] the straight poop." The lawyer has to be someone "who doesn't care what the President thinks of him. His obligation is to tell the President what he doesn't want to hear."

On January 27, 1998, Robert Bennett called me to complain about what I said on television. Bennett kept me on the phone for nearly half an hour telling me that I did not understand his "strategy" in the case and accusing me of "Monday-morning quarterbacking" his decisions.

I asked Bennett a direct question: "Did you ever advise the President that in addition to the option of settling the Jones case, he could simply default on the liability phase of the case?"

Bennett replied that defaulting would have been "ridiculous" and "a stupid idea" and that he would have never recommended it. He also told me that it was the President who did not want to settle the case and that he would never agree to default because other women would "come out of the woodwork."

I asked Bennett what kind of an investigation he had conducted of the Lewinsky matter before he allowed the President to be deposed, and he acknowledged that he simply accepted the President's word, since it was supported by Lewinsky's affidavit. I asked him whether he had ever questioned Lewinsky and he gave a vague response. He did say that he was surprised about the questions asked concerning Lewinsky at the deposition.

I told Bennett exactly what I had said the week before on "Internight," that I strongly believed he had made a mistake by walking his client into a perjury trap and allowing him to get into a swearing contest about his sex life. He assured me that he knew what he was doing and that it would all work to the advantage of his client. I told him I hoped he was right, but that I still thought he had made a mistake.

Seven months later, in August 1998, in the presence of a dozen people on Martha's Vineyard, I asked the President whether Robert Bennett had ever told him that he had the option of defaulting, rather than testifying about his sex life. He said: "Nobody ever told me I could default instead of testifying. I thought I had to testify. Nobody told me about defaulting until just now."

A lawyer owes his client the duty to explain all available legal options, even if he believes that the client will probably reject a given option. Bennett failed in this duty. He now argues, in his own defense, that if Clinton had defaulted the Jones case, many more litigants would have "come out of the woodwork" and sued Clinton in the hope that he would default. This is a fallacious argument for several reasons. First, the statute of limitations would have passed on virtually all allegations arising—as the Jones case did—before Clinton became President. Even more important, the moment it became public—which it quickly did—that the President had offered a $700,000 settlement to Jones, there was more than enough incentive for gold-diggers to come forward and sue. If

Clinton was prepared to pay $700,000 to settle a suit he regarded as utterly frivolous and untrue, no greater incentive would have been added if he defaulted and paid far less.

The sad reality is that Robert Bennett, perhaps in his zeal to chalk up a high-visibility win, failed or neglected to tell the President that this was one case that was better for the client to lose and avoid testifying rather than to win and risk testifying falsely.

Defaulting the Jones case would have resulted in bad headlines the next day—and perhaps for an additional week. But testifying about his sex life resulted in a dangerous threat to the Clinton presidency—a threat which would not materialize for several months. Thus we see another instance of the President making a decision that helped him in the short run—by avoiding the negative headlines of a settlement or default—but hurt him greatly in the long run. It was a pattern that would persist.

The Decision to Issue a Public Denial

On January 26, 1998, President Clinton, with the assistance of Hollywood producer Harry Thomason, decided to make a public statement denying a sexual relationship with Monica Lewinsky. Pointing his finger at the TV camera for emphasis, he said:

> I want you to listen to me. I'm going to say this again. I did
> not have sexual relations with that woman, Miss Lewinsky.
> I never told anybody to lie, not a single time—never. These
> allegations are false. And I need to go back to work for the
> American People.

This statement, made directly to the American public and not under oath, has come back to haunt Clinton. Why did he make it? He was under no legal obligation to make any statement. He could easily have said, as so many others have said, "Since the matter is now the subject of a legal proceeding, my lawyers have advised me to make no public comment about it. I'm sure you understand."

But instead, he issued a firm denial of what he would later have to admit was essentially true: namely, that he did, in fact, have some kind of a sexual encounter with "that woman."

Once again, the President and his advisers opted for the quick fix. They felt that it was necessary to put out the political brushfire that was burning around them. By issuing a firm denial, the President could postpone—perhaps forever— the longer-term consequences of his improper sex and his misleading testimony. At the time he made the statement, the President was probably not aware that Lewinsky had saved the semen-stained dress that would eventually force him to change his story. Without the dress, it would always be a "she said, he said" conflict between the President of the United States and a woman who acknowledges on the Tripp tapes that she frequently lies, and who her own lawyer said is an impressionable woman who sometimes fantasizes.

The President's Decision to Testify on Videotape Before the Starr Grand Jury

On July 28, 1998, Monica Lewinsky's new lawyers struck a deal with Starr under which she was given total immunity in exchange for her cooperation and testimony. On July 29,

1998, the President's lawyer, David Kendall, announced that an agreement had been reached with the Independent Counsel regarding the President's subpoenaed grand jury testimony. The subpoena would be withdrawn; the President would submit voluntarily to four hours of questioning in the White House, in the presence of his own lawyers. In reaching this agreement, the President withdrew his constitutional challenge to the power of a grand jury to compel his testimony. This was a serious constitutional issue, especially since Starr had given Lewinsky total immunity from prosecution. This left Clinton as the primary target of the grand jury. But there is grave doubt whether a sitting President can be indicted or prosecuted. If he cannot, then there is even graver doubt whether it is proper to use a grand jury to gather information for an impeachment. In my view, the President could have leveled a serious challenge, on this and other grounds, against the grand jury subpoena. Such a challenge would have taken at least a year to resolve. In the meantime, he would not have had to testify. Perhaps he would never have had to testify (see Chapter IV).

But the President decided to waive this challenge and to testify "voluntarily." I doubt that his lawyers wanted him to testify, especially since he was not prepared to come completely clean. What I don't know is whether at the time the President made the decision to testify he knew of the existence of the semen-stained dress. There had, of course, been rumors of such a dress over the prior months, but they had been denied by Lewinsky's lawyer. Now Lewinsky had gotten new lawyers, made a deal and was cooperating with the Independent Counsel. The news of the uncleaned dress with a telltale stain became public only after the President made his decision to testify. It is fair to ask whether the President's decision would have been different if he knew about the existence of the dress. It is also fair to ask whether the President's testimony in front of the grand jury would have been different had there been no dress. We don't know.

What we do know is that the President's decision to testify before the Starr grand jury gave the prosecutor an opportunity to trap the President once again into committing perjury—this time not in a live deposition in a dismissed case where the testimony was only marginally relevant, but in a grand jury proceeding where the testimony was central.

It also gave the prosecutor an unprecedented opportunity to videotape the interrogation so that it could be seen by Congress and the public. Again the President was warned about the consequences of testifying untruthfully before a grand jury, where his testimony could not possibly be immaterial.

Again short-term considerations prevailed. First, the President's political advisers urged him to testify. They also urged him to avoid that day's image of the President walking into the courthouse—the so-called "perp walk." The White House agreed, therefore, to the making of a videotape that would later show the President being evasive and perhaps even dishonest. Although the President's videotaped testimony was not as bad as many thought it would be—at least in the short run—it was more damaging in the long run than a walk to the courtroom might have been.

The President's Speech

Within hours of completing his grand jury testimony, President Clinton delivered a brief address to the nation, which he now acknowledges was a mistake. It was neither contrite enough to be an apology, nor sufficiently substantive to justify his attack on Starr. Why did he not wait a day, gather his thoughts, calm down and deliver the kind of speech that might well have provided some degree of closure to the entire Monica Lewinsky scandal? Again short-term considerations prevailed. The White House wanted the next day's news to focus on his speech rather than on his testimony.

Starr's Overreaching, Leaking and Half-Truths

All of President Clinton's mistakes, blunders and miscalculations—serious as they were—would not have led to a possible impeachment if Kenneth Starr had not replaced Robert Fiske as Independent Counsel. Several former Independent Counsels have publicly stated that they would never have sought expansion of their mandate to include the Monica Lewinsky matter, even if they believed it was part of a pattern of buying silence with jobs.[4] (At worst, the "pattern" consisted of two cases: one involving Webster Hubbell and the other Monica Lewinsky, and both allegations have been denied by those to whom the jobs were allegedly promised.) Most Independent Counsels would have recognized the Lewinsky matter for what it was—a sex scandal and not an indictable or impeachable offense. Even if it were indictable, experienced prosecutors exercise discretion and do not investigate every possible crime, because our law books are so full of open-ended crimes that full enforcement of the law would bring our courts to a grinding halt. When Henry Hyde engaged in his "youthful indiscretion"—he was in his forties and his affair went on for four years—adultery was a crime in Illinois. Yet reasonable prosecutors rarely investigated or prosecuted that crime.

Nor would a reasonable prosecutor have cooperated with the Jones lawyers in setting a perjury trap for the President, or in leaking the details of the investigation, or in threatening the mother of the alleged victim, or in filing a referral chock-full of irrelevant hearsay about telephone and cigar sex— while deliberately omitting crucial exculpatory testimony from Lewinsky about the President not having asked her to lie or promising her a job.

Some critics believe that Clinton and Starr deserve each other. But we the people do not deserve to see our delicate system of checks and balances endangered by the reckless actions of two obsessed men.

The Constitutional Crisis and Its Implications for Our System of Governance

We live in an age in which governmental lying has become an art form. The Iran-Contra scandal involved perjury by the former Secretary of Defense and others, which was part of a deliberate White House policy to deceive Congress and circumvent the Constitution. Vietnam and the result-oriented investigation of the assassination of President Kennedy are other examples of cover-ups. Lying and deception are rampant in campaigns, in political fund-raising and in Congress. The Justice Department knowingly encourages law students to lie under oath when it requires them, as a condition of employment, to deny even casual marijuana use while at law school and even in college (and, unfortunately, far too many law students do lie, regarding it as comparable to a sex fib). It is remarkable, therefore, that the lies which now form the basis for a possible impeachment are sex lies growing out of a tawdry series of sexual encounters and a civil lawsuit that was dismissed (see Chapter IV).

There can be little doubt that President Clinton intended to deceive, withhold information from, and mislead the Jones lawyers. In common parlance, he "lied" in his deposition. Certainly if anyone answered questions to a friend in the manner in which Clinton answered the questions put to him by the Jones lawyers, we would call him a liar. But there is a big difference between lying and committing perjury, and even between committing perjury and engaging in an impeachable offense. These differences may be technical, but that is because the law, particularly the criminal law, must be technical if it is to afford the protection of fair warning required by our Constitution.

First, a bit of background on the law of perjury. The leading case on perjury was decided by the Supreme Court in 1973. It is called *Bronston v. United States* (409 U.S. 352). Samuel Bronston testified at a bankruptcy hearing in a manner similar to how Clinton testified at the Jones deposition. Here is the colloquy:

Q. Do *you* have any bank accounts in Swiss banks, Mr. Bronston?

A. No, sir.

Q. Have you *ever*?

A. *The company* had an account there for about six months, in Zurich. [emphasis added]

Here is how the Supreme Court described Bronston's answers:

It is undisputed that for a period of nearly five years, between October 1959 and June 1964, petitioner had a personal bank account at the international Credit Bank in Geneva, Switzerland, into which he made deposits and upon which he drew checks totaling more than $180,000. It is likewise undisputed that petitioner's answers were literally truthful. (I) Petitioner did not at the time of questioning have a Swiss bank account. (II) Bronston Production, Inc., did have the account in Zurich described by petitioner . . . The government's prosecution for perjury went forward on the theory that in order to mislead his questioner, petitioner answered the second question with literal truthfulness but unresponsively addressed his answer to the company's assets and not to his own—thereby implying that he had no personal Swiss bank account at the relevant time.

And here is what the High Court concluded:

It may well be that petitioner's answers were not guileless but were shrewdly calculated to evade. Nevertheless, we [conclude] that any special problems arising from the literally true but unresponsive answer are to be remedied through the "questioner's acuity" and not by a federal perjury prosecution.

It is likely that President Clinton was aware of the Bronston case when he gave his answers at the Jones deposition. It is certain that he was aware of the case when he gave his answers to the Starr grand jury. Indeed, his unpersuasive explanation for why Robert Bennett's statement to the judge in the Jones case may have been accurate sounds like it derived directly from the Bronston case. The prosecutor reminded the President that his lawyer had told Judge Wright that Lewinsky's affidavit meant that "there is absolutely no sex of any kind in any manner, shape or form, with President Clinton." The prosecutor then continued:

That statement is a completely false statement. Whether or not Mr. Bennett knew of your relationship with Ms. Lewinsky, the statement that there was no sex of any kind in any manner, shape or form, with President Clinton, was an utterly false statement. Is that correct?

Clinton responded:

It depends on what the meaning of the word "is" is. If "is" means "is and never has been," that is not—that is one thing. If it means "there is none," that was a completely true statement.

Clinton clearly intended to mislead, evade and be unresponsive without committing perjury. He failed in the former, because he was eventually caught. He may or may not have succeeded in the latter. Since it is unlikely that he will ever be tried for perjury, we will never know for sure. Nor will we know whether he would have gone over the line into incontrovertible perjury if that had been the only way to evade the truth. For example, a good lawyer, knowing Clinton's history, would have asked him whether Lewinsky had ever performed oral sex on him. He could not answer that question in the negative without committing perjury (provided that the answer was "material"[5]). Perhaps he would have refused to answer that question. Perhaps he would have lied. Maybe he was prepared to tell the truth in response to an unambiguous question with no wiggle room. That seems unlikely, but no one can be convicted or impeached on the basis of speculation as to what he might have done.

Were the President to be indicted and tried—either after he leaves office or while serving—for perjury, subornation of perjury and/or obstruction of justice, I believe he would probably be acquitted. On the issue of perjury, the questions were too vague, the answers too ambiguous, the follow-ups too uncertain, the materiality too distant to warrant a conviction beyond a reasonable doubt. On the subornation and obstruction allegations, the testimony is too conflicting, and Lewinsky has sworn that the President never asked her to lie and never promised her a job in exchange for her testimony or silence. Even if there were technical grounds for conviction, jurors— who include ordinary people with sex secrets of their own—are notoriously unwilling to convict for sex lies. They understand that people who engage in forbidden sex typically lie about it. A jury in the District of Columbia would be loath to convict the President—or former President—of trying to keep his sex life private.

But even if Congress concludes that the President is guilty

of a crime, that would not necessarily make him subject to impeachment and removal. An impeachable offense under the Constitution consists only of "Treason, Bribery, or other high Crimes or Misdemeanors." This language has historical meaning that should be interpreted in light of our system of separation of powers. For Congress to have the power to remove an elected President from office—without overwhelming proof that he committed what is unambiguously an impeachable offense—would be to violate the core principle of our system of governance: that the three branches are equal and none is subject to interference by the others—except in extraordinary situations. Impeaching and removing a President is different from impeaching or removing any other governmental official. Just as neither the President nor the courts can remove a Congressman or Senator, so too the Congress may not remove a President—unless the Constitution explicitly authorizes it. We are not a parliamentary democracy, in which the legislature is sovereign. We are a republic in which sovereignty resides in three equal and separate branches, which check and balance each other. Congress too is sworn to uphold the Constitution, and if it impeaches and removes a President for reasons other than those expressly enumerated in Article II, it violates its sworn duty (see Chapter V).

The question therefore remains: What kinds of offenses warrant the extraordinary remedy of legislative removal of a President? The answer must be: an offense that poses a clear and present danger to our body politic—a high public violation of official duty, not a low, private sex scandal, even if it may have included acts that might technically be criminal (though almost never prosecuted). (See Chapter IV.)

There are those who now argue that this case is no longer in the legal sphere; it has moved into the political sphere. The truth is that it is no longer either purely legal or political. It has become a great constitutional matter. Whenever one branch of our government seeks to disempower another branch—and the elected President is the executive branch—a constitutional crisis is in the offing. Impeachment and removal of the President is the most extraordinary remedy known to our system of government. Improperly employed, it is a legislative coup d'etat. And there are no checks or balances in place, since there is no appeal to the courts from impeachment and removal.

Those in Congress who are now pushing for a full-fledged impeachment proceeding against President Clinton are playing with constitutional fire. They see short-term, partisan advantage in exposing the President's mistakes. Like the President, they are guided in their actions by tonight's sound bites, tomorrow's polls and the next election. Perhaps that is in the nature of politicians. But who is looking after the long-term interests of our nation?

These long-term interests—in stability and in the preservation of our constitutional system of checks and balances—would be significantly undermined if Congress were to proceed down the uncharted road toward impeachment and removal of a President for sins and alleged crimes that do not themselves endanger our liberties or our system of government.

Twice before in our history, we have gone down the road to impeachment. In the first case, President Andrew Johnson was impeached by the House, tried by the Senate, and acquitted by a single vote. The verdict of history has strongly condemned that impeachment as partisan, regional and unprincipled. The Radical Republicans, who controlled Congress and fought Johnson's policy of leniency toward the South, passed the Tenure of Office Act to keep Johnson from removing Cabinet members without Congressional approval. When Johnson fired Secretary of War Edwin M. Stanton, arguing that the Act violated the separation of powers, Congress seized on this pretext in an attempt to overthrow an unpopular (and unelected) president who had undertaken policies with which they disagreed.[6]

The second case involved President Nixon, who short-circuited the process by resigning in the face of what he believed was certain impeachment and removal. His crimes went to the essence of what an impeachable offense should be: he subverted the Constitution to his own partisan benefit, and in the process endangered the liberties of all Americans.[7] Even so, when Congress was considering his impeachment, I urged the American Civil Liberties Union to defend his civil liberties. He was treated unfairly when he was named as an indicted co-conspirator by his special prosecutor—a charge against which he had no forum in which to defend himself. But in the end, he did have the right to defend himself in Congress against the impeachment charges—indeed, he was afforded far greater rights than those currently being afforded President Clinton. Eventually Nixon decided that he had no defense, and he resigned.

President Clinton has defenses—both legal and constitutional—and he is right to raise them. His legal defenses to the perjury charges are technical and unpopular. His factual defenses to the obstruction allegations depend on who one believes and how one interprets ambiguous circumstances. But his constitutional defense—that trying to conceal an improper sexual relationship is not what the framers of our Constitution had in mind when they specified the offenses for which a president could be removed from office—is powerful.

The constitutional remedy of removal of a duly elected President is extraordinary. It is intended to be invoked only as a last resort, after all other checks and balances have been exhausted. It is like the fire alarm, or the ax behind the glass that must not be broken except in case of a dire emergency. Just how extraordinary the removal of a President—as distinguished from a judge or other individual—was intended to be may be gleaned from the text of the Constitution itself: "when the President of the United States is tried [by the Senate], the chief justice shall preside." This means that the judicial branch must also be involved in the grave act of undoing a presidential election. It also means that the business of governing must essentially come to a halt while the process of judging the President goes forward. No branch of government is left out of the process: the President is occupied defending himself; the legislature is busy judging; and even the judiciary is without its Chief. Thus, the very decision to go forward with the impeachment and removal of a President is a decision to bring the government to a virtual standstill. Only a dire emergency would justify this allocation of governmental resources away from the important matters of day-to-day governance and to a process that could consume months.[8] Sex lies by a President do not constitute that kind of an emergency. And for Congress to break the glass protecting the mechanism of impeachment in this case would be to shout "fire" in a crowded and dangerous world. It would be among the most irresponsible political actions in our history.

Recent polls suggest that the Republicans' "core constituency"—the Religious Right and its allies—is clamoring for impeachment. Since these are the voters who come to the polling booths, particularly for midterm elections, there is a partisan incentive to champion their demands. But many of these voters wanted Clinton removed even before the Lewinsky scandal broke. In a recent debate with Jerry Falwell, I got the leader of the "moral majority" to admit that he has been out to get Clinton since the 1980s, when he first learned of the then governor's support for a woman's right to a safe abortion. Falwell virtually admitted that the entire Lewinsky matter was nothing more than an excuse for trying to do what he had unsuccessfully tried to do since the 1992 election: get rid of Clinton. That's why Falwell allowed videotapes to be sold on his TV show that claim Clinton was behind the "murder" of Vince Foster. That's why Falwell hoped that Whitewater, Filegate and the Travel Office investigations would lead to Clinton's removal. Now he insists that Clinton must resign over the Lewinsky scandal.

Were President Clinton to accede to these demands, or were Congress to impeach him, a terrible precedent would be established, under which voters who were dissatisfied with the outcome of a presidential election would look to Congress for relief. That is not how our system of coequal branches of government is supposed to work. That is why it is not in the long-term best interests of the country for Clinton to resign. For Clinton to resign in the face of these charges would be for him to legitimate the kind of sexual McCarthyism that has driven this entire episode. Indeed, he has a duty to remain in office, unless he believes he has committed an impeachable offense. If Clinton were to resign in order to avoid further embarrassment, he would once again be placing his short-term interests above the long-term interests of the nation.

President Clinton began this crisis by opting for short-term gratification—sexual, political and public relations—that created long-term problems. Kenneth Starr exacerbated the crisis by his haste to turn a sexual encounter and cover-up into impeachable crimes. Now those who are pushing for impeachment proceedings are placing their short-term partisan advantages ahead of the long-term interests of our nation. But the issue of impeachment transcends the flawed individuals involved on all sides of this tawdry case. We the people have the ultimate responsibility to assure that our future is not mortgaged to the short-term gratification of selfish needs. That is why this issue is so important, and why every American must understand the process that we are now confronting, so that the informed voice of the people—which is the ultimate check in any democracy—may be heard.

CHAPTER I

The Investigation Begins:
Whitewater

President Needs Special Prosecutor
January 1994

The Clinton White House is surely correct in pointing out the hypocrisy and political opportunism of some Republicans who are now gleefully demanding the appointment of a special prosecutor to investigate the Clintons' financial dealings with a failed Arkansas savings and loan. Although the political memory of most Americans—including many media pundits—tends to be measurable in months rather than years, it is difficult to forget the shrill and ultimately successful campaign orchestrated by many Republicans to scuttle the Independent Counsel Act while their party controlled the executive branch of government. Now that the Democrats are in the White House, civic virtue has suddenly returned to those Republicans who have conveniently changed sides and are now calling for a special prosecutor.

Nor are Democrats immune from mirror-image charges of hypocrisy and opportunism. Some Democrats who insisted on the appointments of special prosecutors to investigate allegations of Republican hanky-panky, are now sanctimoniously invoking the separation of powers and the independence of career Justice Department officials, as arguments against the appointment of a special prosecutor in the Clinton matter.

But it is precisely because there is so much hypocrisy and

cynicism on both sides of the aisle that a special prosecutor should be appointed in this case, and that the Independent Counsel Act—with some needed improvements—should be quickly revived and put in place.[1]

It may well be true, as Attorney General Janet Reno has stated, that career prosecutors are not influenced by the political winds of the day. But it is equally true that the public will simply not trust a process in which the subjects of the investigation—in this case the Clintons—have the power to hire, fire, promote and demote those who will be making important decisions about their political and personal futures. The appearance of fairness and equality is almost as important as its reality, especially when the integrity of the President and the First Lady is at issue.

As an experienced criminal lawyer, I understand the reluctance of the White House to surrender control over the delicate fact-gathering process to an outsider who has no political accountability to the President. Were I his lawyer, I might well take the same view. It is likely—though it is too early to know for certain—that a full investigation may well show some gray areas. That is typical of these kinds of cases. It is unlikely that any clear criminal conduct will be provable by a smoking gun. Nor is it likely that a merit badge will be awarded the Clintons for their role in the financial fiasco called Whitewater.

Accordingly, there is a palpable advantage to them in having the Justice Department, rather than a special prosecutor, conduct the investigation. When the Justice Department completes an investigation, it either secures an indictment or it announces that the investigation has been closed. It does not prepare and distribute a public report on its findings. Special prosecutors, on the other hand, generally do prepare and make public what they have found and why they believe it does or does not warrant criminal prosecution.

If I am correct that this may be a gray-area case, in which evidence of improprieties but not of indictable crimes may be found, then the Clintons are far better off with a Justice Department investigation ending with a simple statement that no indictment is being sought. Period. But as President and First Lady, are they entitled to such a simple "thumbs up, thumbs down" decision? Is not the American public entitled to know everything investigators may learn about the financial, political and legal dealings of our President and his wife?

In a half-century that has included a flawed Warren Commission inquiry into a presidential assassination, the plea-bargained resignation of a vice president, the firing of a special prosecutor by a president, the pardoning of a former president by his hand-picked replacement, the pardoning of a former Cabinet member who may have had incriminating information about the president who pardoned him, and other political actions that have made cynics of many voters, it is imperative that the current allegations be investigated without any cloud of conflict of interest.[2] The only way to remove all such clouds is for a special prosecutor to be appointed immediately to conduct a full investigation and to report his or her findings to the American public.

As a Democrat and a Clinton supporter, my hope is that a special prosecutor will find nothing improper, unethical or criminal in the Whitewater mess. As an American, I want the whole truth to emerge so that the voters can judge for themselves. Let there be a full and open investigation, and let the chips fall where they may.

The Ethics of Whitewater
January 1994

Whoever investigates the Whitewater-Madison Guaranty matter should quickly brush up on legal ethics in general and on the Code of Professional Responsibility in particular. The probe will probably turn up no hard evidence of criminal behavior by President Clinton. Even if, as governor, Clinton used his influence to delay the closing of Madison Guaranty Savings & Loan, and even if he did so in exchange for campaign contributions traceable to bank funds—and there is currently no evidence of either—these elusive facts would be virtually impossible to prove.

What might be possible to prove, however, is that the Rose Law Firm, and some of its partners, played fast and loose with the rules of professional conduct. Those rules, with some variations, govern the conduct of lawyers in virtually every state, including Arkansas. One of those rules prohibits lawyers from engaging in conflicts of interest. And the Rose firm's representation of the Federal Deposit Insurance Corporation in its claims against Madison after it previously was the lawyer for Madison appears to constitute a classic conflict of interest.

Exacerbating this conflict may be a letter written by Vincent Foster to the FDIC soliciting the agency's business. In that letter, Foster apparently failed to advise the FDIC of the law firm's prior representation of the bank. If that failure to disclose a material fact was willful, it could constitute fraud. Federal bank regulators are now looking into this matter.

Then there is the potential exposure of the Rose firm to tremendous civil liability if it helped to cover up Madison's shaky financial condition. In recent years, both accounting and law firms have been held liable for failure to disclose adverse financial information about which they knew or should have known. The Rose firm may be particularly vulnerable on this score, because in 1985 Hillary Rodham Clinton and another partner used an audit by Frost and Co. to show that Madison was financially solvent, and then in 1989 another Rose partner sued Madison on behalf of the FDIC, alleging that the audit was bogus. That partner was Webster Hubbell, who is now the No. 3 person in the Justice Department, and whose father-in-law borrowed more than $500,000 from Madison Guaranty and failed to repay it.[3]

At a more general level is the appearance, and perhaps reality, of conflict that always exists when the spouse of a high public official practices law in front of judges, administrators and others whose careers may be influenced by that official. There can be little doubt that clients sought out Hillary Rodham Clinton precisely because her husband was the governor. Regardless of whether the governor actually influenced— directly or indirectly—any decisions in cases in which his wife was counsel, the appearance of influence is inescapable.

Paul Rothstein of Georgetown Law School, a knowledgeable expert on legal ethics, urges "leniency" in this area: "Unless you want to say the wife of an important man can never apply her trade, you've got to be lenient on that. You don't want to disable professional wives from practicing their trade." But many spouses of public officials have made the decision to withdraw from practicing the kind of law that creates the appearance of improper influence. There are many ways of practicing law—both profitably and usefully—without even coming close to the line of impropriety. Hillary Rodham Clinton's practice of law was so close to her husband's base of influence that many will ask just how good a lawyer Mrs. Clinton would have been if her husband had not been the governor.

These and other ethics issues may become the focus of the special prosecutor. I hope he or she will take these issues seriously, not so much to criticize particular individuals for past derelictions but to educate the American public about this relatively hidden but widely practiced genre of elite influence-peddling. Because this form of "cheat elite" is so prevalent among big-city lawyers and law firms, I plan to begin my legal ethics course with a survey of the ethics issues surrounding Whitewater-Madison. My goal is to sensitize law students to the kinds of ethical problems they are likely to encounter when they begin to practice law.

As a Democrat who voted for President Clinton, I wish Bill and Hillary Clinton had been better sensitized to these issues when they studied legal ethics at Yale Law School in the 1970s. I hope that nothing negative turns up against the First Couple. But as a law professor, I understand the importance of a full and open investigation of Whitewater-Madison that will sensitize a generation of future lawyers to the ethical pitfalls of practicing law at the highest levels of government.

Whitewater Enters a Self-Protection Phase
March 1994

Recent Whitewater events mark a new and potentially critical phase in the ongoing investigation. These events include the replacement of Bernard Nussbaum by Lloyd Cutler as White House counsel, the subpoenaing of and testimony by several high-ranking White House officials, a tough memorandum by the deputy White House counsel forbidding the destruction of any documents or evidence, and the announcement of new rules and procedures for meetings and phone calls between the White House and investigative officials.

There are three central aspects to this new phase. The first is that everything now will be done in the open. There will be no more secret actions, such as disappearing files, shredded papers or private meetings. The new rule in the White House will be "Do nothing in private you would not be proud to justify in public."

The second crucial aspect of the new phase is a diminution of loyalty by White House staffers to Bill and Hillary Clinton as individuals, and an increase in loyalty to the institution of the presidency. Lloyd Cutler made that distinction clear when he accepted his new role. He is not Bill's or Hillary's lawyer. They have their own outside lawyer whom they must pay with their own private funds. It is the role of that private lawyer to deal with the substantive issues surrounding Whitewater, Madison, the Rose Law Firm and everything else that took place before the Clintons moved into the White House. Cutler's job is to advise the President as President about legal issues that have arisen since he assumed the presidency. Obviously this is not a bright line, since the precipitating event of the investigation—Vincent Foster's death and the removal of certain files from his office—seems to have implications for what occurred both before and after the beginning of the Clinton presidency.

The third aspect of this new phase is that some White House staffers are beginning to worry more about their own careers and less about the President and First Lady. Nothing moves an ambitious government official to begin thinking about himself and his family more quickly than receiving a subpoena in a criminal investigation. The first thing the recipient of a subpoena generally does is hire a private lawyer. The first thing the lawyer generally does is caution the client to be concerned with his or her own exposure. A visit to a lawyer's office to discuss a grand jury appearance is a sobering experience for those who have been intoxicated with their proximity to the power of the presidency.

The signs of this new emphasis on self-protection are all around. We read such headlines as "Fears Suddenly Ensnare the Staff" and "With Boss Besieged, Gergen Minds Himself."

What does all this really mean to the ongoing investigation and to the Clinton presidency? The answer to that important question depends upon several facts that we simply don't know. The first, of course, is whether there was any wrongdoing attributable to the Clintons, either in Arkansas or in the White House. If there was none, then this has been the worst-handled legal case I have ever seen, since those handling it have certainly created the impression that there must be a great deal to hide. In my thirty years of experience as a criminal-defense lawyer, I have noticed one general distinction between the actions of innocent and guilty clients: the innocent save every scrap of paper in the hope and expectation that somewhere in the boxes of files, bills, phone logs and diaries they will find some proof of their innocence; the guilty, on the other hand, destroy as much as they can, in the fear that somewhere the prosecutor will find something incriminating.

If there was some wrongdoing, the next question is whether all the evidence that could prove it has already been deep-sixed. We will probably never know the answer to that question, since shredded files cannot be recovered. We may learn the general nature of the destroyed files—that is, whether they belonged to Vincent Foster—but we will never learn whether they contained material that could have proved specific wrongdoing.

If there is nothing incriminating to be found—either because it never existed or because it was successfully destroyed—then this new phase will redound to the advantage of the Clintons. If, on the other hand, there exists incriminating evidence, this new phase will almost certainly bring it to the attention of the special counsel, either directly or indirectly. One consequence of the new emphasis on self-protection will be that some staffers will now develop independent relationships with powerful journalists in an effort to garner favorable press for themselves. They will begin leaking, just as "Deep Throat" and others did during Watergate. Some may also begin talking to the prosecutor, as John Dean did during Watergate.

This is bite-your-nails time on Pennsylvania Avenue.

What Happened to Clinton's Privacy?
May 1994

When President Clinton's lawyer, Robert Bennett, correctly pointed out that Europeans cannot understand the obsession of the American media and public with the private lives of our public officials, he told us only half of an interesting story.

Bennett is right that most Europeans could care less about whether their presidents and prime ministers have sexual affairs outside of their marriages. But the reason for this difference is not a function of American-public prurience or media irresponsibility. It is a function of how our presidents— as distinguished from their political leaders—get elected. In most parts of the world, political leaders do not run for office on the basis of their personal lives. In the United States, our presidential candidates do precisely that: it is they who place their family values, their religious values, and indeed their sexual values at issue.

American presidential candidates rarely run on their records or platform alone. They run on their character, their charm, their charisma, their photogenic quality, their wives' popularity and their rapport with the media. Sometimes this "beauty contest" produces surprisingly good results. President John F. Kennedy could never have been elected as a national leader of any other country at his young age and with his meager record of legislative accomplishments. But he was the right man for his time. So, too, Bill Clinton could never have been so quickly thrust into national leadership in any other nation, based on his governorship of a small state. But these men leapfrogged over generations of more experienced politicians on the basis of their good looks, quick wit, charm, intelligence and other personal qualities.

It is not surprising that among the nations of Europe, the English seem to understand best our obsession with the personal foibles of our presidents. They, too, are obsessed with the personal lives of their royal family. They realize that our president—especially when he is as young and charming as a Kennedy or a Clinton—is an uncomfortable combination of their monarch and prime minister. Our first family is more like their royal family than are the families of most European leaders.

Another country that is quickly learning this lesson is Israel. Since its establishment, the Jewish state has had a parliamentary system of selecting its prime minister. Under that system, experienced parliamentary politicians generally worked their way up the hierarchy. No one cared much about their private lives. Now Israel is moving toward popular election for prime minister, and young, charismatic and photogenic candidates—such as Benjamin Netanyahu—are emerging.[4] Not surprisingly, Netanyahu's private life—including an acknowledged extramarital affair—became big news.

President Clinton insists on confiding to the American public the most personal details of his religious beliefs and practices. Such revelations by European politicians would be as unthinkable as the disclosure of what kind of underwear they wear. The Queen does, of course, speak about religion, because an important part of her role is "defender of the faith" in a nation with an established church. But the American president is supposed to be the defender of the Constitution rather than the defender of the faith, as Walter Mondale had to remind President Reagan during the 1984 election campaign, after Reagan constantly invoked his religious beliefs. American presidents should not wear their religion on their sleeves.

American politicians cannot have it both ways. If they seek election on the basis of their religious and family values, they should not be heard to complain when the public and the media hold them to their campaign rhetoric. Only if they eschew reliance on such personal revelations should they be heard to invoke a right to privacy.

The truth is that most of our politicians don't want to keep their personal lives private—so long as making them public helps them win elections. They only want to keep their personal lives private if making them public may cause them to lose. The American voter cannot be expected to accept such selective invocation of the right to "privacy" by their elected officials.

Disclosure Is the Way to Go, Mr. President
December 1995

It is impossible to know whether President Clinton is acting wisely or foolishly in resisting a Senate demand for notes of a 1993 meeting between White House lawyers and the Clintons' personal lawyer—because we don't know the *contents* of the notes. If they contain nothing seriously embarrassing or incriminating, the President would be wise to turn them over, because standing on the "principle" of lawyer-client confidentiality makes it sound like he has something to hide. Few individuals would like to have their lawyers disclose what went on at confidential meetings. Indeed, that is why we have a lawyer-client privilege—to encourage clients to be frank with their lawyers and not be concerned that their confidential communications will be made public.

But the President of the United States and the First Lady are not just ordinary individuals. And therein lies the problem President Clinton faces in resisting the demand of the Senate—and a comparable demand by the Whitewater special prosecutor.

If the meeting was about Mr. and Mrs. Clinton's *personal* business, then there is no great constitutional issue at stake, since the First Family's personal business is treated no differently by the law from other people's personal business. But if

the meeting was about presidential business, then a constitutional issue would be presented by the President's refusal to
comply with a Senate subpoena. But it is not clear that the
President should be claiming any lawyer-client privilege—as
distinguished from executive privilege—since White House
lawyers are public employees who represent *the Presidency*,
not the Clintons. There loyalty is to *the office*, not the incumbent. Indeed if an incumbent is acting against the interests of
the office—as President Nixon was during Watergate—the
White House counsel may have an obligation to blow the
whistle on the incumbent.

The meeting at issue reportedly involved seven lawyers—
four from White House Counsel's Office and three private
lawyers representing the Clintons' personal interests. The purpose of the meeting was to brief the Clintons' personal lawyers
on Whitewater developments. To complicate matters even further, those seeking the notes allege that during this meeting the
White House lawyers may have improperly conveyed confidential governmental information to the private lawyers, thus
crossing the line between the private Clintons and the public
Clintons.

This is a murky legal and ethical area, with few clear rules
or precedents. Former President Ronald Reagan blurred the
line even further by appointing his own *personal* lawyer—
William French Smith—to become Attorney General. Mr.
Smith thus had in his head both confidential information from
the private Mr. Reagan and confidential information from the
public President Reagan.

Whitewater, of course, also crosses that fuzzy line. It
involves private financial actions taken by the Clintons while

they were still in Arkansas, which are alleged to have influenced public actions taken by Governor Clinton, Presidential Candidate Clinton, and perhaps even President Clinton and the First Lady.

To his credit, President Clinton has tried hard to separate the private from the public. He appointed as his Attorney General someone he did not even know before he became President. His White House Counsel have also been distinguished outsiders, though some of the assistant White House Counsel have come from his inner circle. Even his chief private lawyer is an outsider from a respected Washington law firm. Nonetheless, the lines are blurred precisely because Whitewater crosses the barrier between private and public actions.

Some are arguing that the private lawyers waived any lawyer-client privilege that Mr. and Mrs. Clinton may have had when they disclosed private confidences to the public lawyers. But only the *clients* may waive this privilege. Even if the private lawyers improperly disclosed any private confidences—and there is no evidence they did—such unauthorized disclosure would not constitute a waiver.

No lawyer can confidently assure the President how a court case would come out, since the law and the facts are both too murky for accurate prediction. Nor is this a matter of high principle, since it involves private matters mixed with public accusations. There were no great matters of state or governance at stake in the meeting. The public's right to know probably outweighs the President's right to confidentiality in this ambiguous situation.

My advice to the President is to resolve all doubts in favor of disclosure. Unless there is something devastating in the notes, they should be turned over to the Senate. The President cannot win a fight over the lawyer-client privilege. If the courts require him to make disclosure, he must do so, and he will be seen as having lost and having been compelled by the courts. If the courts permit him to refuse disclosure, he will have won a Pyrrhic legal victory, since the public will demand to know what the President is hiding, and will assume the worst, as some already are doing.

Whitewater: Where Do the Clintons Stand?
May 1996

The convictions of Governor Jim Guy Tucker and the McDougals by Independent Counsel Kenneth Starr pose potential problems for the Clintons that transcend the political opportunism of the Al D'Amatos and the Newt Gingrichs of the world. The real danger to them is that one or more of the convicted defendants—who now face serious prison time—will decide to cooperate with the Independent Counsel in exchange for a reduced sentence. Such cooperation can mean the difference between a long prison term and a slap on the wrist.

There is a great temptation for convicted defendants to tell prosecutors what they want to hear. Sometimes this requires creative fiction. Other times it can be accomplished by stretching the truth just a bit, or by describing ambiguous events more clearly than they actually occurred. Often it simply means telling the unpleasant truth about friends and associates.

Professional prosecutors have always been skeptical of "bought witnesses" who try to "trade up" in order to help themselves. One experienced federal prosecutor, now a judge, lectures to prosecutors around the country about the risks inherent in believing such witnesses. He recommends that witnesses who have something to gain by incriminating others should not be used, except as sources of information, and that every bit of information provided by such witnesses should be independently corroborated. This would be a wise rule for the Independent Counsel's Office to follow, in the event that any of the convicted defendants become cooperating witnesses. The same rule should be followed in respect to those defendants currently facing trial, as well as to "targets" and "subjects" of ongoing investigations.

One expected consequence of the Arkansas convictions will be some muscle flexing by the Independent Counsel's Office and some rethinking of options by those who face prosecution. Had Governor Tucker and his codefendants been acquitted by the Arkansas jury, the dynamics would be different. Lawyers for those now under investigation would be able to flex their muscles, because they would have understood that the Independent Counsel could not afford to lose another case. Indeed, it is even possible that the Independent Counsel would have cut back on its investigations and prosecuted only slam-dunk cases against low-level defendants. But now everything is different. The Independent Counsel can afford to take more chances. Defendants will realize that the Independent Counsel is not about to close up shop, and that it may be to their advantage to win the race to the prosecutor's office and be first in line to make a deal.

This "Monty Hall" approach to prosecution—making deals to exchange testimony for prison time—is typical in political cases involving a hierarchy of suspected criminals. Defendants who are lower on the hierarchy of power are given cushy offers to incriminate those higher on the political food chain. Indeed, one of the well-known "rules" among law violators in this country is "always to commit your crimes with people more important than you are, so that you can trade up." There is, of course, no one more important to the Independent Counsel than President Clinton. There is the grave danger, therefore, that someone will be tempted to make up, or exaggerate, a story about the President in order to curry favor with the Independent Counsel. There is the even greater danger that the highly political Independent Counsel may be willing to believe a story that is not entirely true. Remember, this is an Independent Counsel's office that has elevated the politically motivated leak to an art form, even though it is improper to disclose what has taken place in front of grand juries. There are good reasons for wondering whether the Independent Counsel will exercise an appropriate degree of skepticism toward witnesses who seek to buy their way out of prison by offering testimony against the President or the First Lady. Even if the Independent Counsel decides not to prosecute on the basis of uncorroborated testimony of witnesses-for-hire, there may still be leaks of the questionable testimony, calculated to embarrass the White House.

The jurors in the Arkansas case seem to have applied the rule of caution toward cooperating witnesses, insofar as they rejected testimony by David Hale. One juror characterized Hale as an "unmitigated liar." Another said, "We didn't believe a thing Hale said." Yet another witness said she considered Hale's testimony only when she could corroborate it by documentary evidence or the testimony of a credible witness.

The Independent Counsel has said that the jurors in Arkansas have spoken. Now he must listen carefully to what they said. They disbelieved his cooperating witness. They believed President Clinton. They based their convictions primarily on documentary evidence and the testimony of witnesses who had nothing to gain from their testimony. Unless Mr. Starr has an airtight documentary case against the President—which is highly unlikely—he ought not to wallow in the muck of sleazy witnesses seeking to buy their way out of prison by creative cooperation.

Rule of Law:
Whitewater and the Rewards of Testimony
September 1996

The "Judicial Watch"—a conservative legal think tank—has accused President Bill Clinton of violating the federal "witness tampering" and "bribery" statutes. They claim that the President committed a crime when he "brazenly announced [last week] that he would either pay or raise the legal fees necessary to compensate" witnesses who have incurred substantial expenses as a result of having been subpoenaed by Congressional committees and the Independent Counsel in Whitewater-related investigations. Larry Klayman, general counsel of Judicial Watch, cites the following provision of federal law in support of his serious accusation: "Whoever directly or indirectly, corruptly gives, offers, or promises anything of value to any person . . . with intent to influence the testimony [of that] person" is subject to a fine, imprisonment and disqualification from "holding any office . . . under the United States." Klayman has called for an investigation of what he says is a *"prima facie* violation of the witness tampering and bribery laws of the United States."

There will be no such investigation, and for an important reason that raises broad policy questions regarding the widespread practice of both prosecutors and potential defendants making promises to witnesses "with intent to influence [their] testimony." Prosecutors throughout the country make such promises every day to potential witnesses, intending to influence their testimony. They promise them reduced sentences, get-out-of-jail-free cards, even cash payments, in exchange for their testimony inculpating other, more "important" suspects. Honest prosecutors will acknowledge that the promises and deals they make are often calculated to influence testimony, but they will tell you that their only goal is to influence the witness "to tell the truth." Without such inducements, they point out, reluctant or fearful witnesses will lie or slant the truth in favor of their friends or accomplices. With such inducements, they will simply tell the truth.

It is interesting that this is precisely what the White House Counsel's Office is saying about President Clinton's controversial "promise." The President offered his assistance in the context of expressing his concern that some innocent people may "plead guilty in the face of the special prosecutor because they can't afford to defend themselves." He said he feels "terrible about the completely innocent middle-class people who have been wrecked financially" by being subpoenaed repeatedly by the D'Amato Committee and the Independent Prosecutor's grand jury, and that he was "going to help them pay for their legal bills if it's the last thing I ever do. . . . " When I asked the White House Counsel's office to explain this apparent promise, their spokesperson said, "Our position all along has been firm and clear: people should tell the truth. If they do, we have nothing to worry about."

That, of course, is what prosecutors always say when they

make promises to witnesses in exchange for their testimony: "All we are interested in is the truth."

The problem, as all experienced lawyers know, is that the truth is not always black and white. It often comes in muted shades of gray, especially in cases like Whitewater, where slight enhancements of recollection about subjective states of mind could change an innocent transaction into a culpable one. Contrast the inducements that are now almost certainly being offered James McDougal by Whitewater prosecutors with the "promise" made by Clinton. McDougal is facing years of imprisonment after his recent Arkansas conviction. His former wife, Susan, who was more peripheral to the scheme, received a sentence of two years. Jim McDougal can expect an even harsher sentence, unless he now changes what he has already said publicly—namely, that he knows nothing incriminating about the President or the First Lady. Prosecutors have postponed his sentencing explicitly "to influence" his testimony. They are holding this sword of Damocles over his head with one hand and promising him a carrot—in the form of years lopped off his sentence—with the other. Of course, they only want him to tell "the truth," but they want him to tell the prosecution's "truth" rather than President Clinton's "truth."

President Clinton also wants the subpoenaed witnesses "to tell the truth," but he does not want that "truth" to be influenced by threats of prosecution that cannot be defended against because of lack of resources. In that respect, the Clinton promise can be viewed as an inadequate effort at trying to level a playing field that will always be tilted heavily in favor of prosecutors, since a prosecutor can generally deliver far more than a defendant can ever promise.

President Clinton did not violate any laws when he made his promise to try to help his friends pay their legal bills. Laws are interpreted not only by reference to their literal language but also against the background of existing practices, and—for better or worse—the practice of paying the legal bills of witnesses is widespread among corporate defendants as well as political defendants. In any event, President Clinton's promise was made openly, not "corruptly." It was no more or less intended to influence witnesses to tell the truth than the daily promises made by prosecutors, including the Whitewater Independent Counsel. There is no prosecutor who can cast the first stone when it comes to making promises to influence witnesses. That is why there will be no investigation of the charges made by the Judicial Watch.

Indeed the federal courts have approved far more specific promises by prosecutors, so long as they were later disclosed to the jury. In a Supreme Court decision rendered in the mid-1980s, the defendant learned—after he was convicted—that the United States government has a printed form entitled "Contract for purchase of information and payment of lump sum therefore." The contract promises to "purchase evidence" from witnesses, and monetary payment for the witness to "testify against the violator in federal court." In consideration for these services, "the United States will pay to said vendor a sum commensurate with services and information rendered." The Court concluded in that case that the prospect of "a reward" had been held out to the witnesses if their information and testimony led to "the accomplishment of the objective sought to be obtained . . . to the satisfaction of [the government]"—a euphemism for the conviction of the defendant. The Court found that a reward dangled in front of the witnesses gave them "a personal stake" in the defendant's conviction. It also found that the contingent nature of the government's contract to pay them "served only to strengthen any incentive to testify falsely in order to secure a conviction." Despite this incentive, none of the Justices criticized the government for making this deal. Their criticism was limited to the government's failure to disclose it to the jury. If prosecutors can properly promise large cash payments to witnesses who testify in a manner helpful to securing convictions, then surely it cannot be a crime for a potential subject of an investigation—even if he is the President—to promise to pay the legal fees of witnesses who tell the truth.

The publicity surrounding President Clinton's promise to help pay his friends' legal bills should focus attention on the broader question of *both* sides offering witnesses inducements "to tell the truth." But to accuse the President of witness tampering, without saying a word about the far more pervasive problem of prosecutorial promises—as the Judicial Watch has done—is to engage in one-sided Clinton bashing, unworthy of any legal think tank.

CHAPTER II

Guarding the Guardians:
Do We Need
an Independent Counsel?

The New Independent Counsel Is a Partisan
August 1994

The decision to replace Robert Fiske with Kenneth Starr as the new Whitewater Independent Counsel reeks of partisan politics. The stench comes not so much from Mr. Starr himself—who has a reputation as a fair, if somewhat partisan, Republican—as from the judge who presided over the panel which made the decision. Judge David B. Sentelle of the United States Court of Appeals for the District of Columbia is as partisan a Republican right-winger as now sits on the bench. A protégé of Senator Jesse Helms, Sentelle has contributed to making the District of Columbia Court of Appeals a hotbed of partisan politics. Along with former Ed Meese protégé Lawrence Silberman and former Republican Senator James Buckley, the right wing of that court is well-known among lawyers for its partisan approach to cases. Sentelle's opinions are entirely predictable on most issues involving politics and the Constitution.

Judge Sentelle's political background—he was chairman of the Macklenburg Republican Party as well as chairman of the North Carolina Republican Convention—shows him not only as an ideologue on legal issues, but also as a partisan on political events. Moreover, he is on everyone's short list for possible promotion to the Supreme Court—if a Republican were to become president. Since he is in his fifties, his realistic prospect for promotion would be considerably enhanced if President Clinton were to be defeated for re-election in 1996.

The panel that selected Kenneth Starr to replace Robert Fiske was dominated by Judge Sentelle. It was hand-picked by Republican appointee Chief Justice Rehnquist. The man they selected as the new Independent Counsel is a former member of the same court on which Sentelle now serves, and was one of Sentelle's right-wing soulmates on that court. He is a potential Republican candidate for the United States Senate from Virginia. It is not idle speculation to assume that Sentelle hopes that Kenneth Starr will give the Clintons a harder time than would Fiske—who, though a Republican, is essentially nonpolitical. Indeed, when Fiske served on the American Bar Association's Judicial Selection Committee, he incurred the wrath of the Sentelle-Silberman wing of the Republican Party by opposing some right-wing hacks who were nominated to the bench solely because of their extremist ideology.

The object of an independent counsel is indeed independence. It is not partisan score-settling. The reason judges were empowered to select the independent counsel was precisely to avoid the appearance and the reality of partisanship. But the chief justice selected a known partisan to head the selection panel. That partisan then accepted—and now refuses to disclose—secret letters from other partisans. This very partisan process has now produced a partisan prosecutor with his own political ambitions.

Perhaps a permanent office of independent counsel—entirely removed from politics and staffed by long-term professionals—should be established. The courts should stay entirely out of the selection process.

The crowning irony of Judge Sentelle's very political selection of Kenneth Starr may still be down the road. Any cases eventually brought by the Independent Counsel will be appealed to Judge Sentelle's court. The leader of the liberal Democratic wing of that court is Chief Judge Abner Mikva. On October 1, Mikva will succeed Lloyd Cutler as President Clinton's White House counsel.[1]

Let's Investigate the Whitewater Investigator
May 1996

The Whitewater Independent Counsel—Kenneth Starr—is quickly destroying the credibility and integrity that alone justifies having an Independent Counsel. The reason why Presidents and other high officials are investigated by independent counsel, rather than by the Justice Department, is to ensure that politics do not influence the course of the investigations or the decision whether to seek indictments. From the very beginning Kenneth Starr has allowed political considerations, or at least the appearance of such considerations, to influence the Whitewater case.

Starr's very appointment followed a partisan—and highly secretive—selection process generated by several Republican hatchet men, including Lauch Faircloth and Jesse Helms, and finalized by a partisan judge who had been a protégé of these right-wing Senators. Kenneth Starr was expected by those men who urged his selection to be tougher on the Clintons—and hence more partisan—than Robert Fiske, the excellent lawyer and moderate Republican he replaced.

Starr has certainly not disappointed his selectors. He has behaved like a Republican prosecutor out to gain political advantage for his party. How else can anyone explain the series of leaks—really hemorrhages—that have emanated from "sources close to the Whitewater investigation" and "lawyers close to the probe."

These well-orchestrated leaks include the following:

On May 6, 1994, *Newsweek* reported that "sources close to the investigation told *Newsweek* . . . that FBI experts have identified Mrs. Clinton's fingerprints on" Rose Law Firm records.

On April 22, 1996, a "top official with the investigation" told the *New Yorker* that the odds on Hillary Rodham Clinton being indicted were "at least 50–50."

On May 1, 1996, "a lawyer close to the probe" told the Associated Press that the Independent Counsel was questioning "whether there was more to Mrs. Clinton's conversation with McDougal than the First Lady has described," thus suggesting possible perjury.

On February 4, 1996, "two sources close to Starr's probe" told a newspaper that White House personnel saw Vince Foster leave his office carrying his briefcase, just before he shot himself; yet that briefcase ended up back in his White House office.

On January 29, 1996, "sources familiar" with Starr's investigation told another newspaper that Starr had expanded his probe to include possibly improper payments by Clinton's gubernatorial campaigns to black ministers.

These disclosures, whether true or false, are just the most recent in a continuing torrent of leaks emanating from Kenneth Starr's office, all calculated to embarrass the White House and none permissible under the rules governing the confidentiality of ongoing investigations. Nor can Mr. Starr deny personal responsibility for these leaks. His is not a large office in which the chief cannot exercise control over his deputies. Nothing leaks from an office like Starr's without the chief's tacit consent. If there is any doubt that these leaks are orchestrated from the top, just contrast the hemorrhaging since Starr took over with the relative confidentiality that characterized the same office under Robert Fiske.

Why then would a prosecutor, who was truly independent, want to leak information about an ongoing investigation? Leaking of the sort engaged in by Starr's office does not serve any proper prosecutorial purpose. If there is sufficient evidence to indict, there should be indictments. If not, the investigation should conclude with a report clearing those who have been the subjects of the investigation. Orchestrated leaks are designed to serve a political purpose: to embarrass the President and to provide his opponents with ammunition in the upcoming election campaign. That is an improper role for an Independent Counsel to be serving. Indeed, Kenneth Starr himself has acknowledged that the release of "any investigative information by a member of this office . . . would constitute a serious breach of confidentiality." It would also violate the applicable codes of professional responsibility. In a 1994 case, the Supreme Court reiterated that the appropriate response to prosecutorial leaks is disciplining the responsible prosecutor.

The time has come to investigate the investigator. Unfortunately there is no practical mechanism for conducting an inquiry into who is responsible for the leaks attributed to sources within the Independent Counsel's office. The Republican-controlled Congress is hardly likely to conduct a vigorous and impartial investigation. The Democratic Justice Department is not in a position to probe a lawyer who is supposed to be independent of it. Nor are the partisan judges, who appointed Starr to do exactly what he is doing, going to criticize him for leaking confidential information. Finally, the media—which is the willing recipient of these leaks—is unlikely to bite the hand that feeds it. Perhaps what is needed is an independent counsel to investigate the Independent Counsel! As Yogi Berra once put it, "It sounds like déjà vu all over again."[2]

What Is the Attorney General's Job?
December 1996

As Attorney General Janet Reno "twists in the wind," neither fired nor asked to stay on, the time has come to step back and consider the proper role of the nation's chief law enforcement official. Those in the White House who want Reno to leave accuse of her "disloyalty" to the President. Those who want her to remain argue that an Attorney General's loyalty must be to the rule of law rather to the President.

There are, in fact, three groups of lawyers with different legal responsibilities in regard to the President. The Attorney General is a senior Cabinet officer, appointed by the President and confirmed by the Senate. She is an important part of the President's team, when it comes to issues of policy. In that regard she must be loyal to the President. She cannot, for example, support legalization of drugs or oppose the Brady bill in contravention of the President's stated policies on these issues. But she has another important job that goes beyond policy: she must decide who should be investigated, targeted, given immunity and charged with crime. In performing that job, she cannot be loyal to anyone. She must enforce the law fairly, without regard to persons or politics.

The second group of lawyers is the office of Counsel to the President. They, like the Attorney General, are government employees, paid by the citizens to perform a public duty. What is that duty and how does it differ from the duties of the Attorney General? Is the client the Presidency or the incumbent President? Does Bill Clinton have the right to confide in the Counsel to the President, or can the Counsel be required to disclose what the President tells him? If he can confide, is it on the basis of "lawyer-client privilege," or the more amorphous "executive privilege?" What about the First Lady? Is she included within any privilege beyond that afforded all spouses?

The third group are the personal lawyers hired by Bill and Hillary Clinton and paid for by private funds. There is no question that these lawyers must keep confidential anything they learn from their clients under the traditional lawyer-client privilege; but, since they are not part of the White House staff, are they entitled to learn about matters covered by the executive privilege?

These difficult questions pose significant practical problems for the three groups of lawyers with separate but sometimes overlapping responsibilities. They cannot meet together to discuss the President's problems, since they are each covered by different privileges, and if anyone hears information to which they are not supposed to have access, there may be an impropriety or a waiver of privilege. Moreover, neither the President nor "his" lawyers are supposed to learn about ongoing investigations of them or others. The Attorney General may not give "her boss" a "heads up" on what she has learned in her role as chief law enforcement officer. (This is also true of the Secretary of the Treasury in his role as head of the agency that oversees the Secret Service—an organization that both protects the President and investigates certain crimes.)

It is this conflict between the policy and prosecutorial functions of the Attorney General that also gives rise to the need for so many "independent counsel." Because the Attorney General cannot always be trusted to be independent when she is investigating members of her own administration, Congress has created an unwieldy compromise by empowering the courts to appoint independent counsel. This compromise has created all sorts of problems of accountability, of political partisanship and of overzealous advocacy, especially since the dominant judge on the panel that makes the appointments sits on the most partisan and political of courts—namely, the United States Court of Appeals for the District of Columbia.

Nobody benefits from the need to appoint Independent Counsel. The subjects of such investigations are often hounded and bankrupted. The independent counsel have no accountability or continuity. Almost everyone agrees that the Independent Counsel Law is an *evil*; the only dispute is whether it is a *necessary* evil. It is not surprising that headlines around the country this week read "Both Major Parties Want to Improve Law on Counsels" and "Both Parties Push Change in Counsel Law." But tinkering with the details of the Independent Counsel Law will not solve the major problems or address the underlying structural defect in our system. Even Archibald Cox, whose firing by President Nixon stimulated the enactment of the Independent Counsel Law, said, "I have grown increasingly doubtful whether the law can be changed enough to save it from the damage that the politicians of both parties have done to it."

There is no better example of the politicization of the Independent Counsel Law than the appointment of Kenneth Starr

to investigate President Clinton. Starr replaced a truly nonpartisan counsel, Robert Fiske, who had earned a well-
deserved reputation as an independent and nonpartisan prosecutor. That is precisely why he was fired: because the
Republican hatchet men feared that he was too independent—
of them. Instead they wanted one of their own. And they certainly got one—an active Republican, who was thought to be
seeking either political office or a Republican appointment to
the Supreme Court. Whatever the results of the Starr investigation, they will have little credibility with objective observers.

What we have now is the worst of all possible worlds: independent counsel are perceived as Republican hatchet men out
to get Democrats (or, when the Republicans are in power, as
Democratic hatchet men out to get Republicans). The Attorney General is perceived as protecting the President. Although
both these perceptions may be exaggerated, they clearly exist
in the minds of many cynical Americans who long ago stopped
believing that there is any justice in Washington. Only a structural change that divides the current office of Attorney General into two separate jobs will address this problem.

Much of this difficulty is due to the unique role of the
Attorney General in the American system of governance. In
most other countries, there are two *separate* jobs comprising
the responsibilities our Attorney General carries. There is the
minister of justice, which is a cabinet level *policy* position,
with no law enforcement powers. But there is *also* an *attorney
general* or a *director of public prosecutions*, whose role is to
enforce the law by charging and prosecuting defendants.
That position is an apolitical one, usually held by a professional prosecutor with extensive law enforcement experience

and with no accountability to the president or prime minister. In countries with this division of power, there is no need for "Independent Counsel," "special prosecutors" or the like, since the permanent prosecutor is independent.

We should follow the lead of other democracies in creating two separate positions. The Cabinet job, which can retain the constitutional title Attorney General, can be a political and policy position. There would be no danger of the President appointing a political crony, since the Attorney General would not decide whom to investigate or prosecute. That responsibility would be exclusively in the hands of the Director of Public Prosecutions, who would be selected on a nonpartisan basis by a panel of judges or others outside the political process.

The time has come to recognize that the framers of our Constitution made a serious mistake by creating the single office of Attorney General to serve two conflicting functions. We must bring ourselves into the twenty-first century by breaking these two functions into two discreet offices, the way the rest of the democratic world has done. We can begin without tinkering with the Constitution, by simply having Congress create an Independent Office of Public Prosecution within the Justice Department. The director of that office would be a civil servant appointed for a fixed term by the President with the consent of the Senate. By tradition, that person would be outside of politics and an eminent lawyer of great renown and acceptability to both parties. He or she would not be answerable to the Attorney General on issues of prosecutorial policy or on specific cases, and would be removable only for good cause.

It is not certain whether the Constitution would have to be amended to accomplish this change. Article II grants to the President the responsibility to "take care that the laws be faithfully executed," but that responsibility may be delegated—as it has been—to the Attorney General.

If Congress were to pass, and the President sign, a law creating a permanent, nonpartisan office of Director of Public Prosecutions, I believe it would be held constitutional.

If this legislative solution did not pass constitutional muster or did not work for other reasons, it might be necessary to amend the Constitution so as to create an independent prosecutorial office. The Constitution should never be amended except as a last resort, after all other reasonable legislative and administrative solutions have been tried. But the problems of our current Justice Department and its conflicting roles are so serious, and so likely to get even worse, that we must begin to consider new methods for dealing with them.

It is not a matter of personal criticism against the incumbent Attorney General or past holders of this distinguished position. The problem is inherent in the job. It is of course aggravating when the President appoints as Attorney General someone very close to him, as several Presidents have done. But even when the President appoints a distinguished stranger, such as Janet Reno, it is impossible for any one person to perform these conflicting functions without the appearance, and sometimes the reality, of conflict.

A Minister of Justice with no prosecutorial function will be a better Cabinet member. And a Director of Public Prosecution with no Cabinet role will be a better prosecutor.

Who Is Hillary Clinton's Lawyer?
June 1997

I have long been teaching my legal ethics students that when they become government lawyers they should not expect their conversations with other government employees to be as protected by the lawyer-client privilege as would be a conversation between a *private* lawyer and his government-employee client. I was not surprised, therefore, when the United States' Court of Appeals for the Eighth Circuit ruled that Hillary Rodham Clinton's conversations with White House lawyers were not covered by the lawyer-client privilege and that notes of meetings attended by both her own private lawyers and government lawyers would have to be turned over to the Independent Counsel investigating Whitewater-related crimes.

But I was surprised, and disappointed, when the United States Supreme Court denied review of the lower court's decision, because that decision has broad implications—beyond Whitewater—for every government employee who may face investigation. Moreover, there are many other legal ethics experts who were surprised by the Eighth Circuit's decision, and especially by its breadth. This is an issue that cried out for definitive and clear resolution by the nation's highest court. But the Justices these days are cutting back on their docket and denying review in more and more important cases.

The upshot of the High Court's inaction is that the Eighth Circuit's decision—ruling broadly that conversations about possible wrong-doing between government employees and government lawyers are not protected by the lawyer-client privilege—is now the most definitive statement of the law. Although that decision is technically binding only in Arkansas and the handful of other states comprising the Eighth Circuit, every government lawyer throughout the United States will now feel compelled to advise those who seek their counsel that all communications may be subject to subpoena.

The most immediate beneficiaries of this rule will be the private bar in Washington. Since communications between government employees and *private* lawyers remain fully protected by the lawyer-client privilege, government employees will be well advised to confer with private lawyers when they want to ensure that their conversations remain confidential. But private lawyers charge a lot of money, and government employees do not make a lot of money. With today's pervasive atmosphere of scandal, it is only a slight exaggeration to say that every government employee will have to come to Washington with his or her own private lawyer in tow. This may serve as yet another deterrent to government service by good people who know that when they come to Washington they may well be accused of bad things.

Moving from the more general to the particular, it remains to be seen whether the material that has now been turned over to Independent Counsel Kenneth Starr hurts Hillary Rodham Clinton. I doubt that it will. There has been a consistent pattern in the White House of refusing to disclose, litigating, losing and then eventually disclosing material which turns out to be relatively innocuous. Many lawyers wonder why the first instinct of the various White House counsel has been to behave as if there were something to hide. Such an approach may make some sense when a lawyer is representing an ordinary client, but when the subjects of the investigation are the President and the First Lady, it would seem like the better course of conduct would be to disclose everything that is likely to emerge. This White House has chosen instead to litigate and lose—and only then to disclose.

It has been reported that the President and First Lady have been surprised when they have lost in their various legal efforts to postpone or withhold. If that is true, then they have not been receiving very good legal advice. Oliver Wendell Holmes once defined the job of a good lawyer as predicting what the courts will do. Any good lawyer should have advised the Clintons that they would probably lose, and that their refusal to proceed without litigating would be misunderstood as an attempt to cover up crimes or sins. At the very least, the Clinton lawyers should have alerted their clients to the serious risks involved in litigating and losing.

Now the Independent Counsel has a powerful weapon to use against the Clinton White House. The unreviewed precedent of the Eighth Circuit would seem to allow Starr's lawyers—he has just hired four more highly experienced prosecutors—to subpoena other documents in the files of White House lawyers, and perhaps even the lawyers themselves to talk to the grand jury about what the Clintons may have told them or what the lawyers discussed among themselves.

Emboldened by the Supreme Court's inaction, Starr may move aggressively, confident that no court will now interfere with his investigation and that no White House counsel will now recommend withholding or delaying disclosure. The Clintons—and the country—would have been much better off if the disclosures had been made without litigation, which has led to a broad precedent, and even greater uncertainty about the role of government lawyers.

Starr's Conflict
August 1997

So now the Independent Counsel investigating the Clintons may have to have another Independent Counsel appointed to investigate him. A federal judge—a long-time Republican appointed by President Nixon—has written an opinion suggesting that Kenneth Starr may have a conflict of interest in investigating the Clintons. It turns out that Starr has accepted a position as Dean of the School of Law and Public Affairs at Pepperdine University—a job he has postponed but still intends to take. Nothing wrong with that, except that the very school that hired Starr is substantially subsidized by the notorious Clinton-basher Richard Mellon Scaife. Scaife is among the most irresponsible anti-Clinton ideologues, and has made it his life work to see the Clintons disgraced. This is what Judge G. Thomas Eisele has said about the potential conflict: Mr. Scaife, said to be a bitter opponent of President and Mrs. Clinton, especially with respect to Whitewater-related issues, has apparently helped to arrange and make possible the very career opportunities that Mr. Starr wants to pursue as soon as he completes his work as Independent Counsel.

This is not a mere theoretical conflict. It is likely that if Starr were to exculpate the Clintons, he would be making a fool of his benefactor, who has staked his credibility on wild claims of wrongdoing by the Clintons. A newly appointed dean would think long and hard before alienating the major financial supporter of his school. In light of the seriousness of this conflict, Judge Eisele called for the court to assign a lawyer to investigate and report back to the court. But, Judge Eisele added, he alone did not have the power to appoint an independent counsel. Only the court, as a whole, could do so.

Because of the incestuous nature of Arkansas politics, it is unlikely that Judge Eisele's cogent views will receive the support of a majority of the sitting judges in the Eastern District of the state; a number of them have recused themselves from considering the ethics complaint against Kenneth Starr because of their associations with the Clintons. One judge is married to the widow of Vincent Foster, Jr., the former White House lawyer whose suicide was the subject of a Starr investigation. Others were appointed by Clinton and know him personally.

But even if no further action is taken by the court, this broadside by a Republican appointee demonstrates the contemporary relevance of the old Roman question, "Who will guard the guardians?" It is essential that a mechanism be created to oversee the independence of the allegedly independent prosecutors who were appointed to do objective justice. Kenneth Starr's appointment was tainted from the very beginning because he was appointed by a panel of judges dominated by the Republican Right.

Judges should not be in the business of appointing independent counsel, for several important reasons. First, the panel that selected Starr is known for its political and ideological bent. Though judges are supposed to be above politics, too many are still steeped in it.

Moreover, some of the same judges who appointed the Independent Counsel may have to rule on the propriety of his actions. These judges might be reluctant to chastise their own appointee, lest it make them look bad.

A special nonpartisan commission, consisting of retired justices, law school deans and presidents of bar associations—all beyond the age of political ambition—should have the authority to appoint independent counsel, and to assure that they do not engage in the kind of conflict of interest of which Kenneth Starr appears to be guilty.

Checking Starr
February 1998

Which is more dangerous to our liberties: a President who may have had a sexual encounter with a willing intern and then tried to cover it up? Or a prosecutor who may have leaked secret grand jury testimony in an effort to get potential witnesses to change that testimony, and who hid his conflict of interest from the court?

Most Americans correctly believe that the allegations against Kenneth Starr are far more serious, and his alleged misconduct—if it occurred—far more dangerous to our liberties. First, deliberate leaking of grand jury evidence is both against the law and in violation of legal ethics. Second, it undercuts the basis of our constitutionally mandated grand jury system. Finally, a prosecutor who acts as if he were above the law raises the most profound questions of checks and balances.

There are other alleged abuses as well. We now know that Kenneth Starr, before he was appointed Independent Counsel, consulted with Paula Jones's lawyers on legal strategy. And now there are allegations that someone in his law firm—a former Bush and Quayle aide named Richard Porter—may have done even more work for Jones's lawyers. Porter was privy to negative research done by the Bush-Quayle campaign against candidate Clinton and may well have provided such information to the Jones lawyers. Were Starr a judge—as he once was—he would be disqualified from participating in any case that touched on the Jones matter, since he and his law firm helped one side of that case. The rules for an independent counsel should be no different, since he has even more power than a judge. Yet it is doubtful that Starr disclosed his role as a consultant to the Jones lawyers when he sought expansion of his jurisdiction to cover alleged perjury and obstruction of justice in the Jones case. Had he made such disclosure, no objective court would have granted him the expanded authority. He would have been disqualified and someone else appointed to investigate all matters touching the Jones case. That does not mean that *this* court would not have granted him the authority, since its presiding judge—David Sentelle—is a political crony of Jesse Helms, and anything but objective on President Clinton.

Even in the face of these serious questions, there is no process currently available by which to review the alleged improprieties of the Independent Counsel. The Justice Department can't do it, because Starr is supposed to be independent of the administration. The courts are not equipped to conduct the kind of thorough investigation that will get to the bottom of the leaking, because they lack the investigative capacities to interview witnesses and follow evidentiary leads.

But there is a possible solution. The courts could appoint a "special master" to investigate the facts and report back to the judges. This procedure is followed in other kinds of cases, and the courts are deemed to have the power to supervise and investigate matters within their jurisdiction. Surely this power extends to the Independent Counsel, since he was selected by the courts and is subject to their jurisdiction.

There are a few steps Starr himself can take to get to the bottom of the problems in his office. First, he can require every person in his office—lawyers, investigators, staff assistants—to sign a waiver of any journalist privilege, and authorize any journalist who may have received a leak from his office to disclose its source. Second, he could require everyone in his office to sign an affidavit swearing, under penalties of perjury, that he or she did not leak. Anyone who is unwilling to submit to these procedures should be discharged. There can be little doubt that at least some of the leaks—of the content of the FBI wiring of Linda Tripp, for example—had to come from Starr's office. My own suspicion is that after Starr publicly complained that he could not get his story out, someone in the office interpreted that as a subtle request to start leaking.

Finally, Starr could disclose the precise nature of his contacts—and those of everyone else in his law firm—with the Jones lawyers, and also disclose how much, if any, of this he told the court when he sought expansion of his jurisdiction to include the alleged perjury in the Jones case.

Kenneth Starr must be accountable to someone. If, as the Supreme Court has held, the President of the United States is not above the law, surely the Independent Counsel is not above the law. Our system of checks and balances should not tolerate an unchecked prosecutor who may be breaking the law.

Why So Many Crooks at Justice?
May 1998

Kenneth Starr's second indictment against former Associate Attorney General Webster Hubbell—questionable as it may be—raises the perplexing issue of why so many high-ranking Justice Department appointees have themselves been the subject of criminal investigations.

In the past half-century, Truman's Attorney General, J. Howard McGrath, was fired under a cloud after he tried to dismiss a special investigator appointed to inquire into possible improprieties at justice. The head of McGrath's tax division went to prison for conspiracy and tax fraud. Nixon's Attorney General John Mitchell went to jail for obstruction of justice. His deputy, Richard Kleindeinst, received a suspended sentence for his illegal role in Watergate. Reagan's Attorney General Ed Meese, though eventually not prosecuted, was the subject of an Independent Counsel investigation and numerous allegations of wrongdoing. The report of the Independent Counsel was extremely critical of his conduct as Attorney General. And Webster Hubbell pleaded guilty to bilking his clients and now faces trial—along with his wife, his lawyer and his accountant—for tax evasion.

Not a pretty picture of some of those sworn to enforce the law at the highest level. To be sure, there have been many distinguished and law-abiding citizens at the top of the Justice Department, but even a few bad apples in so sensitive a job reinforces the cynicism many Americans have about the fairness and integrity of law enforcement.

All of the Justice Department officials who have come under suspicion of wrongdoing have one characteristic in common: they were political cronies of the President. It is true that not all political cronies who have served in the Justice Department have gotten into trouble; but it is also true that nearly all high-ranking Justice Department officials who have gotten into trouble have been political cronies.

Not surprisingly, most presidents insist on having one of their "cronies" in a high position at Justice in order to protect the President and his loyalists from investigation and prosecution. This situation creates the potential for conflict of interest and outright corruption. It also encourages the President to appoint, as his watchdog, someone who "knows the ropes"—which sometimes means, as it did with Hubbell, someone who plays fast and loose with legal and ethical rules.

It is this potential for conflict and corruption that made it necessary for the United States—again alone among Western democracies—to endure the office of Independent Counsel, with all of its potential for overzealous targeting. Put bluntly, we cannot trust a political appointee and Cabinet member to investigate the President to whom he or she is supposed to be loyal. The history of corruption at the highest levels of justice—episodic and occasional as it has been—underlines this sense of distrust. The result has been the independent counsel, which is itself subject to partisan manipulation, as the appointment of Kenneth Starr demonstrates.

The time has come to take the cronyism and partisan politics out of the Justice Department. This can be done in several ways. The best, but most difficult, change would be to divide the current role of Attorney General into its political and law enforcement components. If this proves unfeasible, then the President should be precluded from appointing cronies to the Justice Department. Following President John Kennedy's appointment of his brother as Attorney General, Congress enacted an anti-nepotism law. It is not possible to draft an anti-cronyism law, but the Senate could refuse to confirm Presidential cronies to any position at the Department of Justice.

A tradition of nonpartisan, non-crony integrity must be demanded for the Department of Justice. If that were to occur, we could dispense with the current necessary evil of the Independent Counsel. More important, we could reduce the cynicism about justice that indictments such as those against Webster Hubbell inevitably generate.

Starr Above the Law
June 1998

Kenneth Starr is acting as if he were above the law. He apparently believes that it is improper for lawyers to invoke entirely lawful procedures that make his biased search for "truth" more difficult. In a recent speech, he did not explicitly mention his current investigation against the President but clearly intended to send a message to Clinton's lawyers and the rest of the criminal defense bar. This is what he said: "Lawyers have a duty not to use their skills to impede the search for truth." He also implicitly threatened lawyers who tried to impede his investigation with obstruction of justice charges, suggesting that such charges might be appropriate even if the alleged impeding took the form of invoking lawful privileges. As an experienced lawyer and judge, he should know better.

Indeed, criminal defense lawyers have an ethical obligation—enshrined in the code of professional responsibility and derived from the Sixth Amendment to the Constitution—to invoke every available legal privilege that serves the interests of their clients. If it is in the interest of a client to invoke the lawyer-client privilege, the husband-wife privilege, the priest-penitent privilege, the lawyer must do so, or risk being guilty of ineffective assistance of counsel. The same is true of the Fourth Amendment, the privilege against self-incrimination, the prohibition on hearsay, or any other exclusionary rules that impede a prosecutor's one-sided search for the truth.

The role of the defense attorney is not to make it easier for the prosecutor to convict his client. The defense lawyer's duty is to his client, not to the prosecutor's "search for truth." Our Bill of Rights was not designed to make the job of prosecuting accused criminals easier. It was designed to strike an appropriate balance between the societal "search for truth" and the preservation of important individual rights, such as privacy, autonomy and zealous representation. The safeguards of our Constitution apply to President and pauper alike. The President is not above the law, but neither is he below the law.

But Kenneth Starr doesn't see it that way. He regards his "search for truth" as an end that justifies any means. So did those who conducted the Inquisition and the Star Chamber. He urges lawyers to be "guided not simply by the client's interest" but by society's interests as well. That is what Stalin expected from Soviet lawyers. Such a rule would require the criminal defense lawyer to serve two masters at the same time, thus creating a conflict of interest. Starr tells the lawyer to say "no to the client . . . we can't argue that." But if the argument is legally and ethically available, and will serve the client's interests, the lawyer has no right to say no. He must argue "that," regardless of how unpalatable "that" may be to his personal taste. The lawyer is acting in a *representational* capacity, not in a *personal* one. He is the client's representative in the legal matter.

The lawyer need not accept the case—unless he is appointed by the court—but if the lawyer does accept the case, he must do *everything* legal and ethical to serve his client's interests, even if that means helping a guilty client to be acquitted.

Starr cites the fictional lawyer Atticus Finch as his paradigm. But Finch had an easy case: his client was innocent. What if Finch's client—a hated black man in a Southern white town—had been guilty? Should Finch have stood up in court and proclaimed his client's guilt? Or what if his client's innocence or guilt were not clear? Should Finch have told the jury that the case was a close one? No, the job of a criminal defense lawyer is to be an advocate for his client's cause. I'm certain Starr recognizes that role when he serves as an advocate for his cigarette clients. I don't remember him disclosing his client's secret in the search for the truth that was being conducted by the plaintiff's lawyers in the cigarette cases. Indeed, the obligation of a criminal defense lawyer to his client is greater—and more rooted in the Constitution—than the obligation of a civil lawyer.

Starr has the right to his personal opinion, wrong and hypocritical as it may be, but he has also begun to threaten lawyers who disagree with him. The threat may be subtle, but coming from a prosecutor it has a chilling effect on zealous advocacy. Starr asks the following pregnant question: "At what point does a lawyer's manipulation of the legal system become an *obstruction* of truth?" The answer should be clear: *only* when the lawyer violates the rules. And no lawyer violates any rules when he employs the rules—including all available privileges and exclusionary rules—in the interest of his client, whether the lawyer believes his client to be innocent, guilty or somewhere in between.

CHAPTER III

The Paula Jones Lawsuit

Individual's Rights Trump Executive Privilege
January 1994

In a ringing proclamation elevating the right of an individual
to redress legal grievances above the power of the president to
be immune from civil liability for unofficial acts, the United
States Court of Appeals for the Eighth Circuit has reversed a
lower court order that would have delayed the trial of Paula
Corbin Jones's sexual harassment suit against Bill Clinton
until his presidency is completed. A divided court noted that
our Constitution "did not create a monarchy." Instead it
established a system under which every individual "is subject
to the same laws that apply to all other members of society."
Accordingly, Jones's federal lawsuit should proceed as any
other private lawsuit would, without regard to the office that
the defendant now holds.

Well, not quite. The court went out of its way to make it
clear that the trial court should schedule the case with sensitivity "to the burdens of the presidency and the demands of the
President's schedule." What this means is that the case will—
in practice if not in theory—proceed on the President's schedule and not on Jones's. It also means that if the President exer-
cises his right to seek rehearing before the entire Eighth Circuit
and then the Supreme Court, even if he loses, the case will not

99

really begin until after the election in November. This, by itself, is a political victory for the President, because it means that no damaging disclosures will be leaked during the campaign. That is probably why he appealed the earlier ruling, which delayed the trial itself until after his presidency but allowed pretrial discovery to proceed immediately.

Politics aside, the majority decision is correct in principle. It is important for the courts to come down on the side of individual rights when they are pitted against presidential prerogative. Whatever one may think of the credibility and merits of Jones's factual allegations—and I do not put much stock in them—they raise important legal concerns under our civil rights laws. Hers is not a mere run-of-the-mill tort suit, as an automobile accident case would be. She is alleging an abuse of power by a state governor committed under color of law. Congress has legislated a special civil rights cause of action for such claims, recognizing the important public interest involved in holding those in power accountable for private abuses committed under the authority of public trust.

If the court of appeals had sided with the president, it would have created a dangerous and overboard precedent. The President already has immunity for his official actions. It would strike an improper balance to extend that immunity to personal actions as well. For example, if Clinton were to have actually punched columnist William Safire in the nose,[1] as he quite understandably wanted to do, he should have no immunity from that unpresidential but very human act. In this case—if Jones is to be believed, as she must be for purposes of deciding whether she has a right to try to prove her case in court—Clinton is accused of even more serious conduct.

All in all, the appellate court struck the proper balance. It reaffirmed the principle of equal rights for all under our law, while recognizing the reality that the President's schedule must be accorded special deference. The decision vindicates the rule of law while reflecting the role of common sense.

Where Are the Anita Hill Feminists Now?
May 1994

Paula Corbin Jones's suit against President Clinton indeed poses problems for our beleaguered chief executive. But it also raises an embarrassing risk of inconsistency—and hypocrisy—for feminist supporters of Clinton who insisted on a full airing of Anita Hill's allegations against Clarence Thomas.

By any standard, Jones's charges against Clinton are far more serious, have far more corroboration and are far more consistent with other allegations against the alleged perpetrator than were Hill's charges against Thomas. The Hill charges—even taken at their most extreme—were that Thomas had used rude and suggestive language. The Jones charges go well beyond language and include allegations of possible criminal conduct, specifically physical assault and lewdness.

The Hill charges lacked credible contemporaneous corroboration. Jones, on the other hand, says she told several people about Clinton's conduct as soon as it took place, and these people have provided contemporaneous corroboration. Moreover, several state troopers may be subpoenaed to corroborate the circumstances. Hill did not come forward with her charges until nearly a decade had passed. Jones waited less than three years.

Finally, Hill's allegations against Thomas were inconsistent with Thomas's prior conduct and reputation. That cannot be said about Jones's allegations against Clinton. It may well be that Jones made up the entire story, or at least the most salacious parts of it. But it also may well be that Hill made up some or all of her account. The point is, many feminists took the position that women who allege sexual harassment should be believed. Indeed, Anita Hill has been speaking at conferences entitled "Women Tell the Truth." It certainly cannot be the position of the sponsors of these conferences that only liberal women who accuse conservative men tell the truth. When conservative women make allegations against liberal men, these allegations cannot be taken any more or less seriously.

No one can know for certain what took place behind the closed doors of that room in the Excelsior Hotel on May 8, 1991. There are inconsistencies in Jones's story, just as there were in Hill's. Jones and her supporters may have financial and political motivations, but so may Hill and her supporters. One fact is beyond dispute. Hill has made a fortune off speaking and book fees solely on the basis of her accusation.

It is too early to make an informed judgment about the credibility of the Jones allegations. But it is not too early to insist that they must be treated no differently from "politically correct" allegations of sexual harassment made against "politically incorrect" defendants. Charges of sexual harassment are too serious to be allowed to be used selectively, against only certain types of people.

Clinton's lawyer, Robert Bennett, has gotten off to a bad start by questioning "whether a sitting President may be sued for alleged events that took place before he entered office." Of course he can. No American is above the law. Just as Vice President Spiro Agnew could be, and indeed was, indicted for conduct that took place before he entered office, so too a President is not above the law of sexual harassment and assault. By questioning whether his client can even be sued, Bennett conveys the impression that he is afraid of putting his client under oath. And perhaps he is.

But the President will almost certainly have to testify under oath—first by depositions and then in court—unless the suit is withdrawn or dismissed. Nor is it likely that a court will dismiss the complaint on legal grounds, since it appears to make out a cause for action and is being filed within the three-year statute of limitations.

It is important to remember that this is merely a lawsuit brought by a single individual. It is not an indictment or a complaint filed by an agency. Like the suit brought against Cardinal Joseph Bernardin, it may prove baseless.[2] Certainly the President is entitled to the same presumption of innocence that protects anyone charged with any misdeed. But as the world awaits Clinton's response, it also awaits the response of those feminists who did not accord Thomas any presumption of innocence, and who—in other cases—adopt the knee-jerk attitude that "women tell the truth." Some do and some don't—as is true of every type of allegation.

Jones's accusations should remind us how easy it is these days to level the thermonuclear charge of sexual harassment. Whichever way this case comes out, it should serve as an object lesson on why those accused of so heinous an offense should not be presumed guilty just because some feminists believe that "women tell the truth."

Should Jones v. Clinton Be Postponed?
May 1994

There will be no trial in the case of *Paula Jones vs. William Clinton* before the next presidential election. That much is certain. Simply by having his lawyer, Robert Bennett, raise the claim of executive immunity in the case of alleged private actions before he became President, Clinton has succeeded in postponing any trial for at least two and a half years. Even if the trial judge were to rule against the claim of executive immunity, that could be appealed, first in the United States Court of Appeals and then the Supreme Court, before any trial were ordered.

Although in ordinary cases appeals generally can't be taken until after completion of the trial, the Supreme Court has created a special exception for claims of immunity. This exception makes good sense, since the claim of immunity goes to the very issue of whether there can be a trial; requiring that the trial be conducted before the immunity claim is resolved would moot that important issue.

The process of briefing and arguing the immunity issue in three separate courts will take years, and even if President Clinton were, in the end, to lose, no trial could realistically be scheduled until after the 1996 election at the earliest.

It is possible that Clinton may succeed in receiving a ruling that defers any trial until after he leaves the presidency. That is surely the most he can realistically expect. No court would grant a President total and permanent immunity for all private torts, contract violations and other civil wrongs— no matter how egregious—that he may have committed as a private citizen (or state officeholder). Such a ruling would fly in the face of our legal tradition that no person is above the law—a tradition that distinguishes the American presidency from the British monarchy.

Election to the presidency does not wipe the slate clean and deny claimants the right to secure legal remedies. But election to the presidency may very well make the incumbent unanswerable to the usual legal processes of the civil courts. That is the issue Bennett has raised, with the support of the Justice Department.

In assessing this issue, there are four different scenarios that must be considered. The most compelling case for immunity is when a President is sued during his presidency for official acts done during his presidency. The law is clear for this scenario: there is absolute and permanent immunity.

The second most compelling case is when a President is sued after his presidency for official acts done during his presidency. The Supreme Court has ruled, in a 5–4 decision, that under that scenario, too, the President has absolute and permanent immunity. The reason for such immunity is that a President should not be burdened with the prospect that his official actions will be second-guessed by juries after the fact.

The third most compelling case is when a President is sued while in office for nonofficial acts—say, sexual harassment— done during his presidency. There is no clear decision for this scenario. The courts might well conclude that the difficulty of distinguishing the official from the nonofficial acts of a sitting President is too daunting and political a question to resolve, and thus will extend the immunity to cover all acts done by a President during his presidency (subject, of course, to the impeachment remedy).

That leaves us with the current scenario: a sitting President being sued during his presidency for nonofficial acts done before his presidency. Under this scenario, the only issue is the toll that such a lawsuit would take on the time and energy of the incumbent.

There is a rational, middle-ground solution to this difficulty. The courts should not impose any kind of immunity on the President. They should allow most of the preparation for the suit to go forward. All other witnesses should be deposed. All motions and other legal issues should be argued. But a temporary stay should be issued for all aspects of the suit that realistically require the extensive personal involvement of the President, such as making his own deposition.

The trial itself would thus be postponed until after the President has left office, but it would be ready to commence shortly after he has returned to civilian life. That is the way a lawsuit would be handled if, for example, a defendant became seriously ill for a period of time. Such a compromise would strike an appropriate balance between the legitimate demands of the presidency and the equally legitimate demands of our system, which holds that no person can be placed above the law.

President Clinton should not ask for more than this, and if he does, the courts should not grant it.

The Paula Jones Charade
January 1997

Paula Jones's lawsuit against President Clinton will never come to trial—not while Clinton is President and not after he leaves office. That much is absolutely certain. The variable is when the case will be settled. If Paula Jones were to win a complete victory in the Supreme Court, requiring the President to submit to depositions now, the case would be settled now. If President Clinton were to win a complete victory, postponing all depositions until he was out of office, the case would be settled after he leaves office.

The most likely result is a compromise, under which parts of the case could go forward now but without requiring the President himself to submit to lengthy and time-consuming legal proceedings. Such a result would permit the President to defer settlement until after he leaves office, when the negative publicity would be slightly muted.

Why do I believe the case will never go to trial, and will be settled? Because that result is the least risky for both sides. No lawyer worth his salt would allow the President to be asked whether he ever used state troopers to arrange dates for him. Even if the truthful answer to that question is no, it would put the President into a swearing match with state troopers that could expose him to a perjury prosecution. Moreover, no Pres-

108

ident or ex-President will allow the office of the presidency to be soiled by submitting his "private parts" to judicial examination so that it could be determined whether they match Paula Jones's alleged description. So, you can take it to the bank that Bill Clinton will not subject himself to the indignities and risks of the pretrial discovery process. He certainly will never subject himself to a public trial at which these issues would be aired, perhaps even on television.

Why then will Paula Jones settle the case? Because she and her lawyers know that if the case were to go to trial, she would almost certainly lose. Jurors will be understandably skeptical about her story that the Governor of Arkansas and candidate for President of the United States simply dropped his pants and exposed himself to a woman who indicated no prior willingness to participate in a consensual sexual encounter. They will remember that—according to her own account—she willingly went into a hotel room with the governor after being told that she "made his knees knock." Even if the jurors credit most of what she and her corroborating witnesses have said, they will probably conclude that whatever may have happened in that hotel room was entirely consensual. They will also believe that upon leaving, she realized that her friends had seen her—an engaged woman—go up to the hotel room of a man who said she made his knees knock. Accordingly, they will probably find that she told her friends she had rebuffed the advances of the governor, when she had, in fact, welcomed them.

Even if a majority of the jurors were to credit her entire story—an unlikely prospect—they would still be hard-pressed to find significant damages to a woman who went into a hotel room with a man who she knew had a sexual interest in her. They will know that she did not even file suit until a newspaper reported that a woman named Paula had engaged in consensual sex with Clinton. It was this disclosure, not anything that happened in the room, that she claims damaged her, and the disclosure did not come from Clinton. These are the realities of how jurors think about these matters, even in 1997, and her experienced lawyers know that they can do much better with a settlement than with a jury trial.

The Justices also understand that this case will never come to trial. Nevertheless, the abstract constitutional issue before the High Court is an important one, because it could affect future suits against incumbent presidents. Justice Sandra Day O'Connor hit the nail directly on the head with a perceptive hypothetical. She asked what should happen if a President were to be divorced and there were a custody dispute—would the children's interests have to await the completion of the President's two terms? On the other side is the question of whether every local trial judge should have the power to overrule the President's schedule and require him (or her) to submit to the court's schedule—as judges routinely do with other busy people.

In the end, the Court will rule that the President is not above the law, but it will protect the President's ability to function without interference from the courts. The bottom line for President Clinton is that the case will be settled more favorably to him, and on a better time line for him. But it will be settled.

The Supreme Court Is Right in the Jones Case
June 1997

The Supreme Court got it just right in ruling that President Clinton has no constitutional immunity, as Chief Executive, from responding to a lawsuit brought against him by Paula Jones. Our American President, unlike a European monarch, is not above the law. The Supreme Court had previously ruled that the late President Richard Nixon had to comply with a subpoena for White House tapes. That was a harder case because the tapes contained Oval Office conversations that may have involved confidential issues of state. This case involved alleged private conduct that took place in an Arkansas hotel before Clinton became president.

The High Court's ruling, while a theoretical victory for the rule of law, is not a total practical defeat for President Clinton. It contains the following important language:

> A stay of either the trial or [pretrial fact-finding] might be justified by considerations that do not require the recognition of any constitutional immunity . . . The high respect that is owed to the office of the chief executive, though not justifying a rule of categorical immunity, is a matter that should inform the conduct of the entire proceeding.

This language gives the President's lawyers some wiggle room in which to maneuver. It means that we will not see President Clinton sitting down for deposition anytime soon. His lawyers will seek delay after delay from the trial judge— they always do. Some postponements will be granted—they always are. When the trial judge finally runs out of patience—they always do—and sets a firm date for the deposition, the defendant's lawyers will appeal, citing the above quoted language from the Supreme Court. This will delay D-day (deposition day) even further. The goal of the President's lawyers will be to delay D-day until after Clinton has left the presidency. If that were to succeed, the case could be settled more quietly, outside the glare of the White House. It can never be settled in the way some cases are settled—with a total confidentiality agreement. Even former Presidents are deemed accountable to the public for their actions, and the terms of any settlement will eventually be disclosed.

Let there be no mistake about the reality that this case will be settled. It will never come to trial, nor will it ever reach the deposition stage. President Clinton's lawyers will not allow him to get into a swearing contest with Paula Jones, with Arkansas State Troopers, or with other witnesses who might contradict him. Remember that pretrial depositions are extraordinarily open-ended. Objections on grounds that a question is irrelevant are rarely sustained. Clinton could almost certainly be asked whether he ever used state troopers to introduce him to women, whether he committed adultery with anyone during the time period at issue, or whether he was alone with Paula Jones in the hotel room. He could also be asked about the alleged unique characteristics of his private parts. No lawyer worth his salt would allow the President to respond to such questions. So the case will be settled, even if Jones's allegations are untrue. The only question is when.

Paula Jones's lawyers may try to press their Supreme Court victory quickly, by sending the President a series of simple written questions—called interrogatories—for immediate response. It could contain only a few basic questions for which little preparation is needed. For example, "Did you ever have any state trooper ask a woman to meet privately with you?" Clinton's lawyers will not allow him to answer that question. But if the first batch of questions are kept simple and short, they will be hard-pressed to demand long delays in responding. Any request for repeated delays to such interrogatories would put Jones's lawyers in a good position to claim that the requested delays are being sought for improper tactical or political reasons, rather than for legitimate scheduling reasons.

The President's lawyers will renew the settlement talks that broke down on the eve of the filing of the lawsuit. If negotiations fail, the President's lawyers could try to bypass the issue of liability—either by not disputing it or defaulting by their failure to respond to pretrial discovery—and move right to the issue of damages. This would then focus on Jones rather than Clinton. But it would be a risky strategy, because it would create the public impression that Clinton was acknowledging that he did it.

A better strategy would be to pay some money, without acknowledging liability, and claim that it was being done in the interest of getting back to the business of running the country.

The bottom line is that the Supreme Court decision is very good for the country, pretty good for Paula Jones and pretty bad—but far from fatal—for Bill Clinton. Just how bad it will be for Clinton depends on how well his lawyers play the mediocre cards they have been dealt.

Are Clinton's Lawyers the Problem?
January 1998

The hardest decision that lawyers have to make is whether to recommend settling a case or litigating it. The recent expansion of Independent Counsel Kenneth Starr's investigation of President Clinton into the Monica Lewinsky matter seems to suggest that the President's lawyers may have made the wrong decision in not settling the Paula Jones case at the earliest possible time. It is impossible to know, of course, what the President's lawyers recommended, and whether the President accepted or rejected any recommendation that they may have made. But the virtue of settling the Paula Jones case early would have been the removal of any incentive on the part of Jones's lawyers to dig more deeply into other allegations of Presidential misconduct.

The presumption of innocence must be applied as strongly to a president as to any other citizen. Just as the President is not above the law, so too he is not beneath our strong constitutional presumption of innocence. In addition to this presumption, there is good reason for disbelieving anything said by Monica Lewinsky, since she either lied in her affidavit or in her taped conversations with Linda R. Tripp. As Robert Bennett, the President's lawyer, correctly pointed out, the ongoing lawsuit by Paula Jones creates incentives for lying and exaggerating by those out to get the President. But that is precisely why this case should have been settled earlier—before these incentives blossomed into full-blown accusations and an unseemly and dangerous swearing contest.

In general, it does not appear as if the President has been well-served by his lawyers, though it is possible that he has made it difficult for them to serve him well. It is always difficult to second-guess the job a lawyer is doing without knowing the whole truth. We, of course, do not know the whole truth. But nor, I suspect, do the President's lawyers. In my experience, it is a rare client who is completely candid with his lawyer. This is true of clients who are entirely innocent, as well as those who may be guilty or in gray areas. But what we do know is that the President has been made to appear guilty by some of the tactics undertaken by his lawyers. If he is in fact innocent, then his lawyers have not served him well. But if he is guilty, then his lawyers may have served him well by making him *appear* guilty without any solid proof emerging. My own strong suspicion is that he is far more innocent than his lawyers have made him appear.

The White House and its large array of political and legal advisers have failed to understand the basic message of Watergate and other legal-political scandals. That message is that the cover-up is always more damaging than what is covered up. If the most recent allegations turn out to be of any merit—and I continue to presume that they will not—then this will once again demonstrate the importance of that lesson. The public does not seem to care whether the President did or did not have an inappropriate relationship with a White House intern. If he did, he certainly would not be the first president to have crossed that line. We should presume that he is innocent of that charge. But the far more serious allegation is that he may have urged his accuser to lie. I doubt that happened, but the mere fact that it is being plausibly alleged demonstrates the dangers of covering up—or even appearing to cover up.

Imagine how different the President's position would be if, right from the beginning, he had urged his lawyers to let the truth come out, whatever the political damage might be. I believe he still would have been elected, and he would be free of any legal problems. President Clinton is an extraordinary politician. I believe he is able to withstand virtually any political attack. But he is not above the law. If he put his legal situation at risk in order to enhance his political situation, he made a serious mistake, because no politician—regardless of how able—can withstand the probings of a determined prosecutor armed with evidence. I believe that the president and his lawyers have increased the likelihood that if incriminating evidence exists, the special prosecutor will eventually get his hands on it.

It is still not too late to settle the Paula Jones case. The cost of such a settlement—both financial and political—will be much higher now than it would have been had a settlement occurred earlier. But the stakes are much greater now, and the reasons for settling are much more compelling.

President Clinton's place in history may well be influenced by what he and his lawyers decide in the next few weeks. I hope they make the right decisions.

Clinton Should Have Settled the Jones Case
April 1998

Despite his stunning legal victory in the Paula Jones lawsuit, President Clinton would have been much better off had he settled or even defaulted the case before being required to testify under oath about his sex life. Judge Wright's decision did not establish that Paula Jones was lying when she accused then Governor Clinton of improper actions. Only a jury trial could have established that, as I believe a jury trial in this case probably would have. Instead the President got a technical legal victory, merely establishing that if he did what he was accused of doing, it did not constitute sexual harassment as a matter of law.

But by the time he achieved this victory, it had come at a very high price. He had put his presidency in the hands of a partisan and overzealous Independent Counsel. By allowing his client to testify under oath, Robert Bennett gave Kenneth Starr the biggest gift of his life—an excuse for continuing and expanding his never-ending criminal investigation. I do not believe that President Clinton should or will be impeached. But I do believe that his continuing problems stem largely from his lawyer Robert Bennett's decision to go forward with depositions, when he could have avoided these depositions by either settling or defaulting the case. Bennett turned a political problem, which was within Clinton's power to control, into a legal disaster that is beyond Clinton's power to control.

For those who think that Bennett's strategy helped the President, consider the following question. Would the President have been better off settling or defaulting the Jones case six months ago and incurring two or three days of negative press, or "winning" the case after swearing under oath to facts that are contradicted by the taped statements of Monica Lewinsky? It seems clear to me, and to most lawyers I know, that settling or defaulting a civil case—especially one where the damages would have been insubstantial—is preferable to risking criminal investigation.

The nation and the law would also have benefited from an early settlement of the Jones case. The nation would have been spared the spectacle of a President testifying about his sex life. The White House would have been able to devote its full attention to the nation's other problems. And the law of sexual harassment would not have been as badly distorted as Judge Wright was required to distort it in order to reach the just result she reached. I believe that President Clinton was not guilty of sexual harassment because he did not do the things Paula Jones said he did. But I find it hard to agree with some of the reasoning in Judge Wright's opinion. The opinion says that "a supervisor's mere threat or promise of job-related harm or benefits in exchange for sexual favors does not constitute quid pro quo harassment." As I read this statement, it seems to suggest that if a supervisor gropes an employee and asks for sex, promising favors if she submits and threatening consequences if she does not, this is not against the law unless the employee either agrees to have sex or the supervisor carries through with his threats. But if the employee does not sleep with the supervisor and the supervisor does not actually punish her, the threat alone does not constitute sexual harassment. Though there is some case law to support that view of sexual harassment, it seems wrong. An employer who threatens reprisal against an employee who refuses to sleep with him should be deemed guilty of sexual harassment. If current law does not agree, it should be changed.

This is an example of a hard case that made bad law. I suspect that Judge Wright did not believe Paula Jones. Indeed, she explicitly refused to credit an affidavit submitted by Jones's lawyers claiming that she suffered severe emotional distress and "consequent sexual aversion." But she did not have the power to dismiss this case on the ground that she disbelieved the plaintiff. Her only power was to dismiss the case on legal grounds. The consequence is a disquieting opinion that lies around like a loaded gun, ready to be used as a precedent by real sexual harassers who use their position as supervisors to try to extort sex from employees.

All in all, the Clinton victory in the Paula Jones case may prove in the end to be Pyrrhic. It has helped Clinton politically, but he didn't need much help in that arena. His poll numbers have remained high throughout this uncomfortable episode. The President is left with a rejuvenated criminal investigation that would probably have ended by now were it not for Starr's windfall in obtaining the President's sworn testimony about Lewinsky. All of this could have been avoided if the President's lawyer had known where to pick his battles.

CHAPTER IV

Monica Lewinsky:
Is It About Sex or
About Lying About Sex?

Subornation of Perjury: But by Whom?
January 1998

The questionable law enforcement techniques being employed by Kenneth Starr against President Clinton should be a cause of concern to all Americans, regardless of their politics or feelings about the President.

By threatening to prosecute Monica Lewinsky and her mother unless the former intern gives him the story he wants, Starr may well be encouraging Lewinsky to bend—or even break—the truth. Lewinsky knows that without transactional immunity, she could be prosecuted for past perjury, since her sworn affidavit is apparently different from what she said on the tapes. The president's lawyers do not have the power to rescue her from this jeopardy. Indeed, they cannot offer her anything—or even talk to her. Starr can offer her full immunity. But he will not do so unless her story is consistent with what he wants to prove. Otherwise, he will prosecute her—though his mandate does not extend to alleged perjury committed in the course of a civil case unrelated to Whitewater. This kind of one-sided bargaining power gives Starr the strength of the legendary godfather—to make an offer that cannot be refused. He can point to Susan McDougal as an example of someone who spurned his offer and is now languishing in prison.

Every experienced criminal lawyer knows what kind of testimony this brand of coercion can produce: a story tailored to secure the desired immunity without regard to whether that story is true, false or somewhere in between. The law books are filled with cases in which immunized witnesses lied because they believed that the prosecutor would give them immunity only in exchange for a story that helped him get a higher-up. I have had several clients who were tempted to stretch the truth in order to get a better deal. In at least one case, a client tried to invent an elaborate story against a public official in exchange for his freedom. Fortunately, when pressed by his lawyers, he admitted that the story was false and that he made it up because it was the only way he would save himself from imprisonment.

The risk that a prosecutor, like Kenneth Starr, could induce a false story from a frightened target is greatest when the allegations against the higher-up are vague. Crimes such as "subornation of perjury" and "obstruction of justice" are as vague as they get. A slight shift in nuance or emphasis could turn the true reality of an innocent conversation or job offer into the false memory of an apparent felony. The shift in nuance need not even be deliberate. Memories tend to be enhanced by the realities of threat and promise.

If Kenneth Starr were really interested in getting at the truth, he would immediately give Monica Lewinsky transactional immunity without *first* requiring her to proffer an incriminating story against the President. He could then compel her to testify in front of the grand jury. If she testifies that the President did no wrong, the immunity would still protect her from being prosecuted for any *past* crimes, but if Starr could prove that she lied in front of the grand jury, the immunity would not protect her from perjury charges for *that* testimony. There is no *valid* reason therefore for Starr to demand a proffer that incriminates the President before he grants Lewinsky immunity. The only reason for this hardball tactic is to influence the *content* of what she will say.

If a defense lawyer were ever to try to influence the testimony of a witness by threats or promises, he would be prosecuted for obstruction of justice—even if he coerced the witness to tell the truth. But prosecutors are not subject to the same rules.

Monica Lewinsky should be free to testify to the truth as she sees it, subject to the usual sanction of perjury, if it can be proved beyond a reasonable doubt that she deliberately lied after receiving the immunity. The content of her testimony should in no way be influenced by Starr's threats or promises. It is not Kenneth Starr who will be testifying. It is Monica Lewinsky, and Starr's heavy thumb should not be on the scales of truth.

Starr's defenders will surely argue that what he is doing—coercing incriminating testimony—is business as usual for prosecutors. That does not make it right—against either the president or an ordinary citizen. The rules should be the same for prosecutors and defense attorneys: neither should be allowed to offer benefits or threaten harms in order to influence testimony. Imagine the irony if a witness in a criminal case were offered something far more valuable than a job—her freedom—in order to induce her to testify that she was offered a job in exchange for her testimony in a civil case.

Can Bought Witnesses Be Trusted?
May 1997

Jurors in the Oklahoma City bombing trial were faced with a dilemma that plagues jurors in countless cases throughout the world. Should they believe the testimony of an alleged accomplice to the defendant, when that accomplice has been given a deal in exchange for testimony? Lori Fortier is only the most recent in a long line of government star witnesses who are colloquially referred to as "flipped," "bought," "rented," "turncoat," "rat," "fink," "snitch" and "cooperating" witnesses. Her story is all too typical. A "close friend" of Timothy McVeigh (he served as best man at her wedding to Michael Fortier, who is also expected to testify for the government), Lori Fortier at first said she believed McVeigh was "in no way responsible for this crime." Now she has completely changed her tune, swearing that as soon as she learned of the explosion at the Oklahoma federal building, she believed it was done by McVeigh, because McVeigh had told her in advance of his plans and had even demonstrated with soup cans.

What accounts for such a dramatic shift in her story? Everyone agrees that it is the deal the government offered her and her husband. In exchange for her "truthful" testimony, she will not be prosecuted for anything, and her husband, in exchange for his, will be prosecuted only for minor charges to which he already pleaded guilty and awaits sentencing. No one believes that she or her husband simply had a change of heart. Indeed, the government acknowledges that but for the deal, the Fortiers would not have become cooperating witnesses. The dispute between the prosecutors and the defense attorneys is over the implications to be drawn from this exchange of testimony for the dropping or reduction of charges.

The prosecutors argue—quite plausibly—that the Fortiers now have a giant incentive to tell the truth, since the deal is dependent on the truthfulness of their testimony. Under the deal, they can be prosecuted for perjury if they lie, and the prosecutors point to several cases in which cooperating witnesses have, in fact, been sent to prison for perjury. Prosecutors also made sure that Lori Fortier told the jury that they had given her "one directive" during the twenty-five hours of preparation for her testimony. That directive was "Always tell the truth."

The defense argues—also quite plausibly—that the very same prosecutors who are trying to convict and execute McVeigh are the ones who will decide whether Fortier is telling the truth. As Stephen Jones, McVeigh's chief defense lawyer, asked rhetorically: "Who decides if you tell the truth? It's the government's truth, isn't it?" The defense will try to persuade the jury that "bought" witnesses, such as the Fortiers, will shape their testimony to the government's needs, even without prosecutors explicitly telling them to do so. These witnesses realize that testimony exculpating the defendant is worthless to the prosecution. The only testimony that will buy their freedom or a reduced sentence is testimony inculpating the defendant.

It is widely believed, by prosecutors and defense attorneys alike, that potential witnesses crawl out from under every rock in a big case, offering the most damning testimony against high-profile defendants in exchange for a deal. Most of these offers are rejected outright by ethical prosecutors, because they are transparently concocted out of whole cloth. But some have indicia of credibility, especially when they can be corroborated to some degree by objective evidence. But even external corroboration is no guarantee of reliability when the witness is clever and calculating. I have seen such witnesses weave their accounts around *existing* external evidence so as to make it *appear* that the external evidence corroborates their testimony. Only when the corroborating evidence could not have been known to the witnesses does it provide an assurance of credibility.

Another complaint made by defense attorneys is that *they* are precluded by law from offering anything of value to a reluctant witness in order to obtain exculpatory testimony. Only the prosecution may buy testimony. And the prosecution may offer life itself—in potential capital cases—as the price for favorable testimony. It may also offer cash incentives, protection, jobs and years of freedom. The defense may not try to level the playing field by making counteroffers; nor can it grant immunity of any kind.

It is the job of the jury to distinguish between "bought" testimony that is credible and "bought" testimony that is incredible. Jurors are generally suspicious of uncorroborated testimony that is the product of a deal, especially when it conflicts with statements made by the same witness prior to the deal. It remains to be seen whether the corroborating evidence produced by the government in the Oklahoma City case will be sufficiently independent to lend credibility to the testimony of the Fortiers. Without such independent corroboration, the testimony of bought witnesses should always be viewed with skepticism sufficient to raise a reasonable doubt.

Buying Testimony
July 1998

If a recent United States Court of Appeals decision were
applied literally to cases around the country, thousands of
federal inmates would be freed—and their places in prison
would be taken by thousands of current and former federal
prosecutors. In the case of *United States vs. Sonia Singleton*,
the Tenth Circuit Court of Appeals—with jurisdiction over
Colorado, Kansas, Oklahoma, New Mexico, Utah and
Wyoming—ruled that prosecutors who offer their witnesses
anything of value, including the likelihood of a reduced sentence, have committed the federal crime of bribing a witness.
Under the terms of this ruling, the testimony of such bought
witnesses must be suppressed and any conviction based on
such testimony must be reversed. The implications of this
unanimous ruling by a relatively conservative three-judge
panel are earth-shattering. The decision has caused a frenzy
of concern in the Justice Department , which has announced
that it will be appealing it to the entire twelve members of the
court. The panel that decided the case has stayed its decision
until it can be considered by the entire court.

If the stay is ultimately lifted, the most immediate impact
of the decision might well be on the convictions of Timothy

McVeigh and Terry Nichols, who were found guilty in the bombing of the federal building in Oklahoma City. Their convictions were based substantially on the testimony of Michael Fortier, an accomplice whose testimony was bought by prosecutors in exchange for leniency. Their cases are now on appeal to the same court that rendered the Singleton judgment. Another case that could be affected by the Singleton decision, were it to be affirmed by the Supreme Court, would be Kenneth Starr's investigation of President Clinton. Under the decision's rationale, Starr's efforts to secure Monica Lewinsky's testimony against the President and others in exchange for leniency would constitute bribery.

The Singleton decision seems correct as a matter of abstract logic and strict statutory construction. The words of the federal bribery statute read as follows: "Whoever . . . directly or indirectly, gives, offers or promises anything of value to any person, for or because of the testimony . . . given or to be given [in a federal case] shall be fined . . . or imprisoned . . . " There are no exceptions in the statutory language for prosecutors or government witnesses. But as Justice Oliver Wendell Holmes taught us, "The life of the law has not been logic; it has been experience." And experience shows that many prosecutions would be made more difficult, and some made impossible, unless prosecutors were free to buy testimony from recalcitrant accomplices. The kinds of cases that would be most affected by the court's new ruling would be conspiracy cases involving organized crime, white collar crimes, government corruption and civil rights violations.

Putting aside the abstract logic and the words of the bribery statute, there are important policy considerations that lend some support to the court's conclusion. It would be strikingly unfair if only the prosecution could buy witnesses but the defense could not. Many potential defense witnesses are also reluctant to testify, fearing government reprisal, dismissal from jobs, embarrassing disclosures, and other unpleasant consequences. Should both sides then be free to offer inducements to testify? Should witnesses be subjected to a bidding war? Of course not. The reason why this would be unthinkable is that he who pays the piper calls the tune. Bought testimony, by either side, places the buyer's thumb on the scales of justice. But that is a good argument against *either* side paying for testimony, and—on balance—that is what the rule should be, even if it makes prosecution more difficult in some important cases. If we take seriously the notion that it is better for ten guilty to go free than for even one innocent to be wrongly convicted, the risks of erroneous convictions are simply too great when the government can buy the testimony of accomplices, especially if such bought testimony is not independently corroborated.

The decision in the Singleton case will have to survive several hurdles if it is to become the law of the land. First, the entire Court of Appeals for the Tenth Circuit will have to agree. If it does, then the case will surely be appealed to the Supreme Court, where the decision will face critical review. Even if it survives that review, Congress has the power to rewrite the bribery statute and exempt federal prosecutors from its coverage. Already some Congressmen are promising to do that.

The Singleton case gives the courts and Congress an opportunity to address the problem of bought testimony in a serious and calibrated manner. Even if they ultimately conclude that the Tenth Circuit went too far, it has surely done a great service by alerting the public to a serious problem in the administration of criminal justice.

Amateur Hour as Lewinsky Defense
February 1998

Monica Lewinsky's choice of William Ginsburg to represent her has disserved not only her interests, but also the public's interest in truth and fairness. Ginsburg, an amiable malpractice lawyer with no experience in plea bargaining or grand jury practice, has done just about everything wrong from the moment he entered the case.

In approaching Kenneth Starr, hat in hand, he violated the first rule of plea bargaining: come to the negotiation with your strongest case; prepare to defend and to go on the offensive *before* you ask for a deal. Only *after* he showed his cards, and they were spurned, did Mr. Ginsburg say he was beginning to prepare a defense.

By then he had proclaimed that Starr's treatment of his client—particularly his long interrogation of her without a lawyer—was entirely legal. Even if that were correct, it would be foolish for a bargaining lawyer to waive all claims of illegality. And it is a close question. As Professor Stephen Gillars of New York University Law School has observed, "the rule says you can't talk to her at all if she has a lawyer." A bargaining lawyer should keep all of his options open.

Ginsburg was actually in a stronger bargaining position than he believed. Starr does not want to end up with an extremely weak perjury prosecution against a twenty-four-year-old former intern whose testimony was, at best, marginally relevant to the Paula Jones case. Starr needed Lewinsky as a *witness*, not a *defendant*.

Ginsburg may have also waived his client's privilege by selectively disclosing what she told him. Though he repeatedly said he would not "broach" the lawyer-client privilege, this is what he told the world about the alleged semen stain on the dress: "I don't anticipate they are going to find a thing. *Based on what I have been told by Ms. Lewinsky*, they were all clean and fresh." As a result of this disclosure, Ginsburg can now be called before the grand jury and asked what Lewinsky told him regarding the dress. Did she lie when she told Linda Tripp she had a semen-stained dress? Did she lie when she said she would never launder it? If Ginsburg was not authorized by Lewinsky to make the disclosure, he can be disciplined. If he was authorized, then Lewinsky can be asked what she told Ginsburg about the dress.

Ginsburg has stated that if there is corroboration, then Lewinsky's bargaining power is reduced. He has it backwards. Lewinsky's uncorroborated account is worthless, particularly in light of her own admission on the tapes that she has lived a life of lies, and her claims, also on the tapes, which her own lawyer now says are false—for example, that she kept a semen-stained dress. It is only if her story were to be corroborated that Lewinsky's testimony would be useful. In that case, her testimony would be essential, since corroborative evidence standing by itself rarely tells the whole story. She would have to tell the story, which could then be corroborated by external evidence.

Ginsburg has also virtually proclaimed that his client is guilty of something. That has been the tone of his public pleas for immunity. He has also contradicted his clients' statements, acknowledged that she has embellished, and suggested that she would withhold information if given only use immunity.

The upshot is that Kenneth Starr believes he can call the shots. He has threatened Lewinsky with prosecution and has offered her immunity, depending on whether she is prepared to tell the story that he wants her to tell. This kind of pressure increases the possibility that Lewinsky may change her story in order to avoid the threat and gain the benefit. For example, she has given different versions of her alleged meeting with the President on December 28, 1997. In one, the President tells her to lie, while in the other, she characterized the President's words more as a "suggestion and not a directive by any means." Starr wants her to testify as to the first version. Neither may, of course, be true, but Lewinsky would benefit more by telling the story as Starr wants her to.

Ginsburg has enlisted criminal lawyers to assist him in his representation of Lewinsky, but he has been her spokesman and it is in his public statements that his amateurism has hurt Lewinsky. Ginsburg seems to be a quick learner, but you cannot learn-while-you-earn in a case of this complexity. One does not go to a cardiologist to treat a brain tumor, regardless of how smart the cardiologist may be. It is time for Lewinsky to end amateur hour and rely on experienced Washington criminal lawyers who can level the playing field against the overreaching Starr.

Clinton and the Three Stooges
March 1998

Kenneth Starr's ongoing grand jury investigation is probably the most important criminal case in recent American history. Yet its three most visible lawyers have little actual courtroom experience in the trial of criminal cases. And their collective inexperience is showing. Nearly every experienced criminal attorney with whom I have spoken—and they include prosecutors, defense attorneys, Democrats and Republicans—agrees that these three lawyers have handled this important case in a manner bordering on incompetence.

The problems begin with Kenneth Starr, who was appointed Independent Counsel despite the fact that he has never tried a criminal case. He was appointed not because of his credentials as a criminal lawyer—he has none—but rather because of his political credentials as a right-wing ideologue who could be trusted by the likes of Senators Helms and Faircloth to do their partisan bidding. The circumstances of his appointment are highly suspect: the removal of a truly independent lawyer following a lunch meeting between the two right-wing Senators and the right-wing judge—a political protégé of the Senators—who is in charge of the panel that selects Independent Counsel. Starr had consulted with Paula Jones's lawyers before being offered the job as Independent

Counsel and should have declined the appointment on con-
flict-of-interest grounds. But he accepted and his overzealous
actions have destroyed the credibility of his investigation.

Next there is the President's lawyer in the Paula Jones case,
Robert Bennett. He is a major cause of the President's problems. Any experienced criminal lawyer would have settled or
defaulted the Paula Jones case rather than allow his client to
be deposed under oath about his sex life. Instead, he foolishly
led the President into a perjury trap, set by Jones's lawyers and
Starr. Jones's lawyers knew that Monica Lewinsky had said on
tape that she had had a sexual relationship with the President,
but Bennett was not aware of that evidence. He did, of course,
know that there were allegations of a sexual relationship
between the President and Lewinsky, because she had been
subpoenaed. Bennett could not possibly have known whether
these allegations were true or false in whole or in part, or
whether there existed corroborating evidence. Yet, like a rank
amateur, he allowed his client to fall right into the trap. Most
recently, Bennett provoked the Jones lawyers into filing hundreds of pages of documents containing additional allegations
of sexual misconduct. Bennett says he expects to "win" the
Jones case, not realizing that whatever its final outcome, he
has already lost it for his client.

Finally, there is Mr. Amateur Hour himself, William Ginsburg. An old friend of the Lewinsky family, Ginsburg had no
experience as a criminal lawyer, he did not understand the
complexities of immunity, plea bargaining and other esoteric
aspects of negotiating a deal with a federal prosecutor. But
instead of simply helping his friends find an experienced

Washington lawyer and then going home, Ginsburg decided to parlay his friendship with the Lewinskys into his own fifteen minutes of fame. Taking to the airwaves, he destroyed his client's credibility and bargaining powers. He made inconsistent statements on her behalf, disclosed privileged communications, and shocked experienced criminal lawyers by his public ineptitude.

It is distressing that the most important criminal case in memory should have so many bunglers involved. There are, of course, some experienced criminal lawyers behind the scenes. Starr has some excellent prosecutors on his staff. Ginsburg has retained an able local criminal lawyer. And President Clinton's other personal attorney, David Kendall, is a superb and highly experienced criminal lawyer. But it is the visible lawyers who are speaking to the public, and they look and sound like the Three Stooges, as they make mistake after mistake.

When I teach my Harvard Law School course on "Tactics and Ethics in Criminal Proceedings," my students will be able to learn from the mistakes of these lawyers. The first thing I hope they will learn is never to accept a case unless you have experience and a deep knowledge of the subject matter. Just as a podiatrist should never treat a brain tumor, so too a lawyer with little or no experience in criminal trials should never accept a complex criminal case. The ultimate loser will always be the client.

In this case, the first casualty was President Clinton, whose lawyer Robert Bennett turned an easily solvable political problem into a legal crisis by allowing his client to fall into a perjury trap. The second casualty was Monica Lewinsky, whose lawyer's amateurism continues to hurt his client. The final casualty may be justice itself, because Kenneth Starr's overzealous prosecution may make it impossible to bring this case to a fair and just resolution.[1]

Starr Uses McDougal to Get at Lewinsky
May 1998

They tell the story of an emergency room surgeon who was so bad that he once killed two people with a single slice of his scalpel—the patient who had been shot in the stomach and could have been saved by a competent surgeon; and the person who shot the patient and received the death penalty when the patient died. William Ginsburg is a lawyer analogous to that surgeon. When he publicly proclaimed on television that Monica Lewinsky "has no intention of falling on her sword"—that she "will not go to jail like Susan McDougal"—he may have sealed the fate of both Lewinsky and McDougal.

Kenneth Starr's decision to throw a whole shelf of books at McDougal was designed to send a powerful message to Lewinsky. The message is: "You will become another McDougal unless you testify against the President, you will spend your entire youth in prison, and the President will not be able to help you."

It is doubtful that Susan McDougal will succumb to the pressure. To her credit, she has decided to stand up to what she genuinely believes to be abuses by Kenneth Starr. But Ginsburg has already said that Lewinsky will succumb to the threat of imprisonment: "She will do what she has to do given the situation she finds herself in." So why not ratchet up the pressure on Lewinsky by subjecting McDougal to further punishment? This prosecutorial tactic is not only unfair to McDougal and Lewinsky, it is also unfair to the real target of Starr's machinations—President Bill Clinton. Ginsburg has already said—publicly—that what Lewinsky says under oath will be a function of what she is offered and threatened with:

> If the prosecutor elects to give full immunity or a promise not to prosecute, you still tell your story, only in a little more relaxed and comfortable fashion. And maybe the prosecutor can get more details than with someone who is under use immunity.

In other words, she will say what she has to say to save her own skin. The greater the immunity, the more incriminating the testimony. Now that she is being implicitly threatened with multiple prosecutions and prison terms for civil and criminal contempt and obstruction of justice, Starr's hope is that she will sing his tune. That is the stick, and it is a large one. Soon we may see the carrot: an offer of some kind of deal (though not as favorable a deal as she probably could have gotten earlier on had she been represented by a more experienced lawyer).[2]

But what is the real value of testimony induced by this kind of stick and carrot, especially when it comes from a witness whose lawyer has said that the content of her testimony will be influenced by what she is offered? If Lewinsky were now to cooperate with Starr and testify against the President, the President's lawyers would have the right to confront her with her lawyer's public statement, since a lawyer is deemed to be speaking on his client's behalf. Starr knows that Lewinsky's uncorroborated testimony would be worthless in a court of law, but his goal is not to indict the President, but rather to submit a scathing report to Congress. Such a report would be one-sided, with no opportunity for the President's lawyers to cross-examine questionable witnesses like Lewinsky.

Starr may opt for another tactic as well. He may indict Lewinsky in the hope that she could provide hard evidence against Vernon Jordan. Starr would then indict Jordan in the hope that he would incriminate President Clinton. This approach—called "climbing the ladder"—is unlikely to succeed, but it could cause nervousness in the White House.

Finally, Starr could simply indict Lewinsky on charges of conspiracy to obstruct justice, and name President Clinton as an unindicted co-conspirator. This is what the independent counsel did to Richard Nixon in the Watergate case. It would be as unfair to Clinton as it was to Nixon, since an unindicted co-conspirator has no opportunity to defend himself. Starr's thinking might be that a conviction against Lewinsky would send a powerful message to Congress about President Clinton's alleged complicity in a conspiracy to obstruct justice.

If this were to occur, President Clinton's reputation might be in the hands of Lewinsky's primary defense counsel—a malpractice lawyer who has demonstrated an ability to serve his own interests at the expense of his client. On the other hand, an indictment against Lewinsky might be a wake-up call to her and her family that they made a dreadful mistake by allowing so inexperienced a lawyer as Ginsburg to speak for her in public. Maybe she will finally understand the need to hire a first-rate, experienced Washington criminal defense lawyer with good judgment and a willingness to place the client's interests before his own.

President Clinton's Rights
June 1998

There is a great public debate over whether the President of
the United States should be entitled to assert "privileges" that
are available to all citizens. Among these are the Fifth Amendment's privilege against self-incrimination, the lawyer-client
privilege whose source is the Sixth Amendment, and the
spousal privilege.

First, a point about terminology. These are not "privileges"
that can be taken away as easily as they are given. They are
rights, enshrined in the Constitution and statutes, and in the
common law. Second, a point about the realities of the President's situation. Bill Clinton is clearly being targeted by the
Independent Counsel, who is using means more typically associated with attempts to prosecute mafia dons, rather than
political figures. Any lawyer worth his or her salt—and the
President's private lawyers David Kendall and Nicole Selig-
man are great lawyers—would advise a client facing an
overzealous prosecutor to assert all legal rights that are in that
client's best interest. The fact that the target here is the President of the United States should not change that legal advice.

Indeed, the White House has learned a painful lesson from
its mistakes, and the mistakes of those who advised the President, in regard to the Paula Jones case. In that case the Presi-

dent put politics before the law. Political considerations dictated that the President not default or settle the Paula Jones case, lest his actions be deemed an admission of improper behavior. Such an admission would have carried short-term political costs. Instead, President Clinton made the most disastrous decision of his presidency: to contest and ultimately to win the Paula Jones case, thereby giving him a short-term political benefit, but at an extraordinary legal cost. In order to win the case, the president had to subject himself to a wide-ranging deposition about his sex life. During the course of that deposition he denied having sexual relations with Monica Lewinsky. There is no conceivable way that Robert Bennett, the President's lawyer in the Jones case, could have known whether the President had or had not engaged in such relations. Yet, he permitted the President to swear that he did not, even after it should have become clear that Jones's lawyers had evidence to the contrary.

It is this deposition, and alleged steps that may or may not have been taken to obstruct justice in the Jones case, that now drives Kenneth Starr's investigation. All of this could have been avoided had the President asserted his legal right to default the Jones case. Yes, default! Lose the civil case, with its negative political consequences, in order to prevent a criminal investigation with far greater legal consequences.

The lesson the White House has learned since the Paula Jones fiasco is that the President has little to fear politically. He can survive the political slings and arrows and emerge stronger for them. He has little to fear from the media, the electorate or even from Congress. What he does have to fear is Kenneth

Starr's investigation and the *legal* consequences that may result from it. The President's major fear is that he himself could be indicted. There is no way of predicting how the Supreme Court would come down on whether a sitting President can be indicted for alleged crimes committed while in office. Another fear is that Monica Lewinsky could be indicted and the President called as an eyewitness. Clinton might have to invoke his privilege against self-incrimination. There will be those who argue that a President should never invoke a privilege against self-incrimination, lest it be deemed an implicit admission of guilt. But when a President is being treated like a potential criminal by an independent prosecutor, he is entitled to invoke the rights that our Constitution grants people in that situation. Moreover, there are circumstances in which an innocent person can and should invoke his privilege against self-incrimination. These include the situation in which an overzealous prosecutor gets a witness to change her story so as to give false testimony that contradicts the true testimony of the target.

These rights should not be invoked frivolously, when there is no conceivable possibility of success. But the rights at issue here are important rights, and their invocation in the context of this case raises close questions. For example, the application of the lawyer-client privilege to dead clients or to government employees and government lawyers raises difficult and important issues. No lawyer should be embarrassed to raise these issues, even if he loses in the end.

Our Constitution bestows inalienable rights upon every citizen who is the possible target of a criminal prosecution.

Just as the President is not above the law, neither is he below the law. He is entitled to invoke every right that serves his legal interests. He should do so without fear of the political consequences.

How Clinton Is Worse Than Nixon
June 1998

There I was, watching the State of the Union, rooting for Bill Clinton to make the greatest speech of his life. The world, too, was watching, hoping he would say something about Monica Lewinsky and the sex scandal swirling around him. When Clinton talked brilliantly about education reform, social security and the budget, I knew why I supported him for President. When he talked passionately about better child care for working parents, I knew why I liked him as a friend. But then he said something that made me explode with anger toward the man I voted for, admired and liked. He talked about saving our "disintegrating 'American' treasures," such as the Bill of Rights. The President was referring, of course, to the *physical* preservation of the original document written in 1793. But the symbolism was grating. Here was the President—who had done more to destroy the *values* reflected in the Bill of Rights than any President in recent memory— shedding crocodile tears about an old piece of paper.

Talk about elevating form over substance! I got angrier and angrier as I began to tick off in my mind what the Clinton Administration had done to trash nearly every right in that disintegrating document of liberty.

The First Amendment was nearly turned into a dinosaur

by the Clinton Administration's support of the Communications Decency Act, which would have stripped the Internet—which will be our dominant means of communication in the twenty-first century—of constitutional protection. Under that benighted piece of legislation, cyber-censors would have had the power to imprison citizens who transmit or receive "indecent" or "patently offensive" material, even though such material is generally protected under the First Amendment. Moreover, the indecency or offensiveness of any particular communication would be judged by the standards of the most restrictive "community" capable of receiving it. And since cyberspace is everywhere, this would mean that Jerry Falwell and Pat Robertson would decide what's offensive and what's not for the entire world. Fortunately, for America, the Supreme Court struck down the statute, no thanks to the Clinton Administration, which vigorously defended it.

As I watched the President accept his well-deserved cheers from the assembled dignitaries, I wondered how a man who was himself an anti-war protester could turn out to be a President so insensitive to the First Amendment rights of others. "Freedom of speech for me but not for thee" jumped into my mind.

The same is true of privacy rights. Here is a President who complains bitterly, and understandably, about invasions of his own privacy—including the surreptitious taping of conversations involving his alleged sexual encounters. But this same President has presided over an administration that has run roughshod over the privacy of thousands of Americans by conducting wiretaps at a record-shattering pace, by authorizing random searches of welfare recipients and by threatening to seek the resignation of a federal judge who had the guts to exclude a cache of drugs illegally seized by overzealous cops. (The judge succumbed to the threat and changed his mind!)

Perhaps the most enduring damage this administration has inflicted on our basic constitutional rights has been its virtual destruction of the Writ of Habeas Corpus, which has been part of the common law for nearly a millennium and was deemed so important by our framers as to be included in the body of the Constitution itself. Yet in an effort to pander to the law-and-order mentality of the day—and to show that he is even tougher on criminals than his Republican opponents— President Clinton supported and signed a law limiting habeas corpus even more than reactionary Chief Justice William Rehnquist has advocated. Under the Clinton statute, defendants will have difficulty challenging conviction in federal court even if they can demonstrate that it is based on unconstitutional procedures or insufficient evidence. Put bluntly, this means that *innocent* defendants will go to their deaths— or remain imprisoned—because of absurd legal technicalities. For example, in a recent case, a federal appellate court reversed a district court decision that freed a woman after finding that she was *innocent* and had been deliberately *framed* by Philadelphia-area police and prosecutors. The appellate court did not dispute these findings of a frame-up, but citing restrictions on the Great Writ, the judges sent the innocent woman back to prison on technical grounds. Texas has executed at least two defendants, despite compelling claims of *innocence*. Under the Clinton law, "mere innocence" is not enough to secure a writ of habeas corpus.

On the issue of the death penalty—which under the Clinton Administration has been expanded to more federal crimes than ever before in recent history—I should not have been surprised. When he was running for President, Bill Clinton stopped his campaign in New Hampshire to return to Arkansas and claim credit for the execution of a man who was so brain-damaged that he tried to order breakfast for the morning after his execution.

And the beat—as in beating up on the Bill of Rights—goes on. Profiling of airline passengers. Mandatory v-chips. Denial of welfare benefits to convicted drug users. Mandatory minimum sentence for first-time offenders. Opposition to gay marriages. Denial of bail to presumably innocent defendants. Virtually every protection of the Bill of Rights has been diminished under the Presidency of the man who, as governor, opposed Robert Bork's nomination to the Supreme Court on the grounds that Bork's "constitutional theories of individual and civil rights" constituted a "threat." Yet he has turned out to be the presidential equivalent of a judicial Robert Bork on some of these same issues of individual rights.

There is, to be sure, a debate among civil libertarians about President Clinton's record on the Bill of Rights. Some, like liberal Nat Hentoff, argue that he is "the worst civil liberties president since [Richard] Nixon." Others, like *New York Times* columnist Anthony Lewis, claim that this comparison is unfair to Nixon: "Bill Clinton has the worst civil liberties record of any president *in at least 60 years*." Lewis observes that "not even in the worst days of McCarthyism did legislation so trample on individual rights." Attorney Harvey Silverglate, Boston's most prominent civil libertarian, has said that President Clinton "has done more to undermine civil liberties than just about any occupant of the White House in recent memory." Critics of the Clinton civil liberties record cover the entire political spectrum, from the conservative Cato Institute to the centrist Electronic Privacy Information Center to the liberal ACLU.

No one, not even Clinton's most ardent political supporters and friends —among whom I count myself—believes that the President's record on civil liberties is exemplary. I support President Clinton despite, not because of, his record in protecting the Bill of Rights.

Nor have Clinton's judicial appointments reflected sensitivity to civil liberties or individual rights. For the most part they are indistinguishable from President Bush's appointments, except that there are more women and minority nominees. These judges may be more supportive of women's and minority concerns, but there is nothing to suggest that they are more sensitive to freedom of speech, defendant's rights, privacy or other unpopular individual liberties that do not have constituencies behind them. As journalist Carl Rowan summarized the situation: "Federal judges are the ones who are leading or countenancing this retreat from our historic protection of civil liberties and privacy rights."

The Clinton Administration has been particularly insensitive to the rights of small, unpopular and uninfluential groups such as criminal defendants, particularly those on death row. So too with alleged pornographers, especially child pornographers. The administration changed its position in midstream as to whether noncommercial home photographs of clothed teenagers in "provocative" poses constituted kiddy porn punishable by years in prison. Succumbing to pressures from the religious right, it successfully urged the Supreme Court to read the child pornography statute so broadly as to include such photographs. It also invoked child pornography as its rationale for upholding the Communications Decency Act, which would have imposed a pervasive regime of censorship on the information superhighway. Nothing, it seems, is too restrictive, if it is done in the name of protecting children or crime victims.

Clinton's occasional defenders point to his support of religious expression and of abortion rights. But these are *majority* rights supported by most Americans, and Clinton's support of them helps him win votes. So does his advocacy of affirmative action without quotas, and his middle-ground position—"don't ask, don't tell"—on gay rights in the military. His defenders point to only one civil liberties position Clinton has taken—opposition to a constitutional amendment prohibiting flag burning—that may have been politically unpopular, though he did support *statutory* restrictions on flag burning—thus cutting the civil liberties baby in half once again. Still they claim that his overall record on civil liberties is "not that bad." This reminds me of the response the former mayor of Jersey City made to a statement from the local Bishop that the political corruption in that city was an "abomination unto the Lord." The mayor replied, "I don't think it's that much of an abomination."

But many believe that the Clinton record on civil liberties *is* that much of an abomination, especially coming as it does from a former professor of constitutional law and a graduate of Yale Law School. Nat Hentoff has called it a "catastrophe." Anthony Lewis has characterized it as "appalling." Phillip

Galey has said it is "scary." Tim Lynch, assistant director of the Cato Institute Center for Constitutional Studies, calls it "a total disaster." John Heilman describes it as "breathtaking in both the breadth and the depth of its awfulness." And the *Progressive* magazine says that Clinton's record on civil liberties makes "congressional Republicans look like card carrying members of the ACLU." First Amendment lawyer Floyd Abrams summed it up this way: "Lee Atwater would have admired it; Dick Morris may yet claim credit for it; Clinton should know better."

Why then would a president who came into the White House with a background that made him appear to be a civil libertarian's dream turn out to be such a nightmare for constitutional rights?

There is a simple answer and a more complex one. The simple answer is that President Clinton is a pragmatic politician who makes decision by putting his finger in the air to determine which way the winds of public opinion are blowing—and the winds always blow against civil liberties. Anthony Lewis espouses that view: "Clinton will not stand on principle when he thinks he might be damaged politically. In the end, he is interested in only one thing: his own survival." Little Rock journalist Paul Greenberg echoes this sentiment: "There is no Bill Clinton. That is, he has no principles he will stand by if they lose him popularity."

It is tempting to accept this simple characterization of Clinton as a political opportunist. But it is an incomplete explanation of why Clinton—who is no more opportunistic than most other politicians—has been so much more insensitive to civil liberties. The answer, I believe, goes far beyond

Bill Clinton as an individual, and is much more ominous for the future of the Bill of Rights as we enter the next millennium. To understand Bill Clinton's dismal record on civil liberties requires an understanding of Bill Clinton's generation—a generation that will likely provide our next president and our future legislators and our future Supreme Court Justices and lower court judges. It is a disturbing and pervasive picture that bodes ill for our fundamental liberties over the next generation.

The story begins in the least likely place—the liberal academy. Over the past quarter century an intellectual war has raged on university campuses between left-wing advocates of women's rights and minority rights on the one hand, and advocates of civil liberties on the other. Many cause-oriented feminists and minority activists see freedom of speech—and civil liberties in general—as a barrier to achieving power. They "know" the truth and tend to be intolerant of the right of others to express "counter-truths" or "politically incorrect" views. These impatient left-wing advocates are winning, and their academic victory is being translated into political policy. The translation is not a difficult one, because left-wing political causes—such as abortion rights, gay rights and affirmative action—bring votes along with them. Civil liberties, however, do not have a significant constituency. Moreover, on some issues—particularly those affecting freedom of speech—the radical left has joined into a censorial coalition with the religious right. The end result is that civil liberties has become bad politics, while the anti-civil liberties agenda is a political freebie.

But that has always been true. Why then is it different

today? Because the liberal academy could previously be counted on to stand up for the principles of civil liberties, no matter how unpopular these liberties might be. Remember McCarthyism and the strong stand against its abuses taken by many prominent academics, including conservatives such as Dean Erwin Griswold of the Harvard Law School. The same was true during other periods of repression. Not today. Many of today's influential young academics make their reputations by trashing civil liberties as the enemy of progressive causes. I remember the comment of one of my own colleagues when some students demanded that the authors of a sexist satire be disciplined. He sided with the students, saying, "the First Amendment just isn't my thing." Fortunately, a coalition of centrist civil libertarians and moderate conservatives was able to beat back the censorial leftists, and the students escaped discipline. But for an increasing number of academics, the First Amendment and other provisions of the Bill of Rights are just not their "thing."

Had the liberal academy stood firm against the Clinton assault on civil liberties, it would have been more difficult for the President and First Lady to ignore a united front of peers whom they respect. But now they can point to supporters among their peers who agree with their subordination of the Bill of Rights to other political considerations. For example, Mrs. Clinton has pointed to *Tikkun* magazine—a leftist Jewish monthly—and its editor Michael Lerner as her guru. And Lerner has declared religious war on the Bill of Rights and unapologetically engages in old-fashioned McCarthyism against those —including me—who believe in the primacy of civil liberties. He, like many in his generation, do not seem to understand the right of every accused to counsel, and the right of every knave to freedom of speech.

The Clintons are also admirers of the Yale Law School faculty. They both attended Yale Law School, as did I and my son. When I was a student there, the faculty was chock-full of civil libertarians (such as Professors Thomas Emerson, Louis Pollock, Guido Calabresi, Telford Taylor and Ralph Brown). Those giants have all moved on—to judgeships, retirement and civil liberties heaven. They have been succeeded by a generation of law teachers to whom civil liberties is far less central. There are, of course, some civil libertarians on the current Yale Law School faculty, but my son's friends and the sons of my friends who now attend Yale Law School tell me that "it's not what it used to be."

The influence of Catharine MacKinnon has become pervasive within many law school faculties. The high priestess of feminist censorship recently wrote a screed against the First Amendment entitled "Only Words" that would have made Stalin proud. Her thesis is that speech which offends her—she calls it "pornography"—is not speech at all. It is simply "masturbation material." Stalin would have called speech that offended him "counterrevolutionary material." MacKinnon regards those who defend free speech for all as "pornocrats" and "pornographer's lawyers." Stalin would have called us "counterrevolutionaries."

Even more mainstream constitutional scholars now regard civil libertarians as extremists. I have heard freedom of speech referred to as a "fetish." The new vogue is "communitarianism," a fuzzy philosophy which elevates responsibility over rights, and the interests of the majority over the liberties of minorities. They have introduced a new vocabulary of "rights" deliberately calculated to confuse. The classic definition of rights is *negative*—a denial of governmental power to intrude on certain basic liberties. Individuals have rights in relation to the government. This certainly was the understanding of our founding fathers, who drafted the Bill of Rights as a limitation on government: it begins, "Congress shall make no law respecting an establishment of religion, or prohibiting the free exercise thereof; or abridging the freedom of speech, or of the press; or the right of the people peaceably to assemble, and to petition the Government for redress of grievances." But now we hear about "victims' rights," which must be balanced against the rights of accused criminals; the "right to pray," which is intended to trump the right to be free from governmentally imposed religious compulsions; the "right to life," which is a euphemism for preventing women from exercising their right to choose abortion; and the right "to be free from" pornography and other offensive speech. Some even speak of the "right" of a murdered person's relatives to see the murderer executed. This new vocabulary of affirmative "right" turns the classic concept of negative rights by government on its head and shows how easy it is to confuse governmental power with individual rights. Every modern tyrant has talked about the "right of the people" as he put dissenters in prison.

The Clinton Administration has invoked this philosophy and vocabulary, especially when expressing its disdain for the rights of defendants accused of a crime. An administration spokesman has said, "There is no greater civil liberty than to protect our families and children." This is, of course, a cynical manipulation of the English language and of the history of our Bill of Rights. If there were indeed no greater civil liberty than the protection of our family, then it would follow that any means—even those prohibited by our Constitution—would justify that noble end. Such a view is a prescription for authoritarianism. The Clinton Administration has gone so far in adopting this phony new vocabulary of "victims' rights" that it has actually championed a new constitutional amendment which it calls the "victims' rights amendment." In reality such an amendment would do little for victims—who often have much in common with perpetrators—but it would seriously undercut the rights of those accused of crime.

The reality, therefore, is that the Clintons are not being hypocritical at all. It is much worse. They really believe this stuff. It was de La Rochefoucauld who described hypocrisy as "the homage that vice pays to virtue." But the Clintons do not regard civil liberties as an unqualified virtue; nor do they regard their curtailment as an unmitigated vice.

Rather, the Clinton Administration's lack of concern for civil liberties is part of a generational attitude that happens to coincide with its political strategy. It will be no better under our next President, whether he or she is Al Gore or a Republican of the same generation. If anything, Gore will probably be worse. His wife has been far more outspoken in favor of censorship than either of the Clintons has ever been. And there is no evidence of any real concern for classic liberties by Vice President Gore, Speaker Gingrich or any other leading political figures of that generation.

Even the American Civil Liberties Union—our traditional bastion against those who would attack the Bill of Rights—is not what it used to be. Some of its leaders have gotten soft on the First Amendment, especially when its exercise conflicts with the ACLU's liberal political agenda. Political issues such as affirmative action and abortion rights have come to dominate the agenda of the ACLU—and for an understandable reason: it is easier to raise funds by appealing to causes with large constituencies, like abortion rights, than to causes with small constituencies, like freedom of speech. When the editors of the right-wing *Dartmouth Review* were being disciplined for expressing racist, sexist and anti-Semitic views, the ACLU's silence was deafening.

There is, perhaps, some hope that President Clinton's current problems will cause him to reconsider his commitment to the Bill of Rights. I am always told that "a conservative is a liberal who's been mugged." There is some truth to that observation. But it is equally true that a civil libertarian is a conservative who is being investigated by the Independent Counsel.

Even if President Clinton were to come to appreciate the virtues of the Bill of Rights as a result of his own experiences with an overzealous prosecutor, this would only provide short-term relief from the larger generational problem we face. My generation grew up with McCarthyism. We learned to appreciate the values of the Bill of Rights the hard way. Until and unless President Clinton's generation experiences—at first hand—the abuses against which the Bill of Rights was intended to protect, we may be in for a long period during which liberty remains unappreciated.

Who Deserves To Be Defended?
April 1997

Imagine a legal system in which lawyers were equated with the clients they defended and were condemned for representing controversial or despised defendants. Actually, one need not resort to imagination, since history reminds us that less than half a century ago, mainstream lawyers were frightened away from defending alleged communists who faced Congressional witchhunts, blacklisting, criminal trials and even execution. Senator Joseph McCarthy, and the millions of Americans—including many lawyers, law professors and bar association leaders—who supported this attack on "commie-symp lawyers," made it impossible for decent lawyers who despised communism but who supported civil liberties and constitutional rights for all, to defend accused communists without risking their careers.

When Julius and Ethel Rosenberg were accused of being Soviet spies who gave the secret of the atomic bomb to our arch-enemies, they were defended by a communist lawyer with no experience in criminal cases. He provided an inept defense and the result was a terrible miscarriage of justice which has only recently been confirmed by Soviet intelligence sources. It now seems clear that the government framed Ethel Rosenberg in a futile effort to get her husband, who was a minor spy, to disclose the names of his accomplices. There is no assurance that an able and zealous mainstream lawyer could have saved either or both of the Rosenbergs from the electric chair, but we should certainly be left with an uncomfortable feeling that McCarthyite attacks on lawyers may well have contributed to a terrible injustice—and to some very bad law—in that and other cases during the 1940s and 50s.

In many parts of the world, it remains difficult today for a despised defendant to be represented by a mainstream lawyer, because many nations—even Western-style democracies—lack any tradition of apolitical or civil libertarian representation. For example, in Israel, which has an excellent legal system, right-wing lawyers tend to represent right-wingers accused of political crimes, while left-wing lawyers tend to represent left-wingers and Palestinians accused of political crimes. This ideological approach to legal representation creates a circular reality in which lawyers are expected to share the political perspectives of their clients. The result is a bar divided along ideological lines which lacks a neutral commitment to civil liberties for all. A similar situation prevails in France, Italy and some other European countries.

Our nation has been blessed with the tradition of a vigorous bar committed to civil liberties for all, regardless of ideology, politics or the nature of the accusation. John Adams, Abraham Lincoln and Clarence Darrow have come to personify this approach. Adams represented the British soldiers who participated in the Boston Massacre. Lincoln and Darrow represented the widest assortment of clients, ranging from corporations to common criminals to the oppressed. It would be a terrible tragedy if we were to surrender this noble tradition to those who are so certain about their ability to discover truth that they become impatient with the often imperfect processes of justice. It was the great judge Learned Hand who once observed that "the spirit of liberty is the spirit that is not too sure that it is right."

It is a rare case in which absolute truth resides clearly on one side. Most cases contain shades of gray and are matters of degree. That has surely been true of most of the cases in which I have participated over my thirty-five-year career. Even in those which are black and white—either the defendant did it or he did not—there is often room for disagreement, and it is the advocate's role to present the client's perspective zealously within the bounds of law and ethics. It is an extremely rare case in which a lawyer knows for sure that his client is guilty and that there are no mitigating considerations. In most of those cases the lawyer will try to persuade the defendant to enter into a plea bargain.

Having made this general point, it is important to suggest several distinctions among types of legal representation. At the pinnacle of cases which should be defended vigorously without regard to ideology are free speech and criminal cases. Surely those of us who defend the free speech rights of *everyone*— including extremists on the right and left, purveyors of sexual material and newspapers that make mistakes—should not be deemed to approve of the *content* of the material which the government seeks to censor. Those of us who opposed efforts by the town of Skokie to censor Nazis did not sympathize with the Nazis; we opposed censorship even of the most despicable and false ideas. It should be equally obvious that those of us who choose to defend people facing execution or long imprisonment do not sympathize with murder, rape, robbery or corporate crime. We believe in the process of American justice which requires zealous advocacy, scrupulous compliance with constitutional safeguards and the rule of law. We understand that most people brought to trial for serious crimes are factually guilty. Thank goodness for that! Would anyone want to live in a country in which the majority of criminal defendants were innocent? That may be true of Iran and Libya, but it is certainly not true of the United States. And in order to keep it that way, *every* defendant—regardless of their probability of guilt, unpopularity or poverty—must be vigorously defended within the rules of ethics. The scandal is not that the rich *are* zealously defended, it is that the poor and middle class are *not*. More resources should be allocated to defending those who cannot afford to challenge the prosecution and to expose the weaknesses of the evidence against them. There are indeed some innocent people in prison and on death row, and it is no coincidence that most of them are poor and unable to secure adequate effective legal advocacy. That is why I devote half of my time to pro-bono cases. Many other lawyers also do a significant amount of free legal representation, but this is not enough to ensure that no defendant faces execution or long imprisonment without zealous advocacy on their behalf. If lawyers are frightened away from taking on unpopular criminal cases, the already serious problem of inadequate representation will reach crisis proportions. There is no surer way of frightening a young lawyer, who is contemplating the defense of an accused murderer or rapist, than to accuse him or her of being sympathetic to murder or rape.

Of course a lawyer has the legal and ethical option of

declining to represent an unpopular and despised defendant whom he believes to be guilty. The real question is whether it is desirable for the decent lawyer to exercise that option on the basis of the "politically correct" criteria of the day. I believe it is not, because—among other things—it will lead to the demise of civil liberties and to the creation of a bar so divided along ideological lines that the defendants who most need legal representation will be relegated to legal ideologues who often believe that politics and passion are a substitute for preparation and professionalism.

Free speech and criminal cases are different from cases involving only continuing commercial gain from immoral conduct. A lawyer who provides ongoing legal assistance to a cocaine cartel is acting, in effect, as a "consigliori" to a criminal conspiracy. A criminal organization has no legal right to continuous advice as to how to evade arrest and increase illegal profits. Many lawyers regard the cigarette industry as indistinguishable from the "mob" (though recent events surrounding the Ligget Group's deal demonstrate that even cigarette lawyers can sometimes help their clients to do the right thing, even if for self-serving reasons). Corporations which are not facing criminal charges do not have the same Sixth Amendment rights as accused criminals; nor do they have the same First Amendment rights as those confronting government censorship. Still, we are all better off with a legal system under which important rights are not denied anyone without affording them the right to be defended by a zealous advocate. If we move away from the American tradition of lawyers defending those with whom they vehemently disagree—as we temporarily did during the McCarthy period—we weaken our commitment to the rule of law. What is popular today may be despised tomorrow. So beware of an approach which limits advocacy to that which is approved by the standards of political correctness.

A recent case in Massachusetts places limits on a lawyer's discretion to decline a case. A feminist attorney who specializes in representing women in divorce cases refused to represent a male nurse's aide who was seeking financial support from his wealthy wife who was a doctor. The lawyer told the man that she did not accept male clients in divorce cases. A panel of the Massachusetts Commission Against Discrimination ruled against the lawyer stating "that an attorney . . . holding [herself] out as open to the public may not reject a potential client solely on the basis of gender or some other protected class." Obviously this situation is different from one in which a lawyer declines a case on political or ideological grounds, but it does suggest that lawyers are not entirely free to decline cases on *any* ground. Indeed, lawyers in Massachusetts, as in other states, are covered by civil rights and public accommodation laws, some of which prohibit discrimination based on religion, creed and political affiliation. Doctors and dentists are not free to turn away patients who have AIDS or whose politics they despise. It is a fair question to ask why lawyers should have greater freedom to discriminate than do other professionals.

In the end, I hope lawyers will not need laws to tell them that they should represent those most in need of zealous advocacy, without regard to gender, race, ideology, economic situation or popularity. Such an approach will make for a better legal system and a freer America.

Starr's Leak and the President's Response
June 1998

Amidst all the hullabaloo about Kenneth Starr's off-the-record press briefings, one important point is being neglected. Whether Starr's leaks did or did not violate federal law, what he and his office did is standard operating procedure for prosecutors—both federal and state—around the country. Every day, federal prosecutors—many appointed by President Clinton—leak negative information about ongoing investigations. They do so for a variety of reasons: self-aggrandizement; to put pressure on potential witnesses and defendants; to curry favor with the media; to attempt to influence the jury pool; to generate favorable public opinion for their office. They always justify what they are doing by claiming that there are "legitimate" law enforcement purposes behind their leaks. But if the purposes are legitimate, why does the information have to be leaked? Why can't it simply be disclosed in a press release?

For years, federal courts have bemoaned the constant leaks from federal prosecutors, sometimes characterizing them as "hemorrhages." Often the leaks are channeled through FBI agents or other surrogates so as to give the prosecutors plausible deniability in the event they are summoned into court. But the effect is the same; prosecutors too often try their cases in the media, for entirely illegitimate reasons. The media encourages such "trial by press," because it serves their interests as well. This requires defense attorneys to defend their clients in the media, though most defendants would prefer that their names never appear in the press.

Now that President Clinton has himself been victimized by prosecutorial press leaks, perhaps he will do something about the general problem. He can begin by directing his Justice Department to forbid all leaks concerning ongoing investigations and by firing those US Attorneys who make a practice of leaking such information. I can provide him a list of names of such prosecutors, but the Justice Department knows who they are. Indeed the Justice Department itself has been guilty of such leaks and knows how to plug them if it wants to. But it has chosen not to. For this reason it would be entirely inappropriate and hypocritical for the Justice Department to conduct an investigation of Kenneth Starr's leaks. It would be putting the fox in charge of investigating the chickens, since Starr is simply following well-established—if improper—Justice Department practices. What is needed is a truly independent investigation by a lawyer with experience as both a prosecutor and a defense attorney, or perhaps by a former judge who has seen all sides of the issue.

It is unlikely that we will get such an investigation, because press leaks have become an important—if unfair—weapon of prosecution. The White House will continue to complain about prosecutorial press leaks damaging to the President, but it will ignore the more general problem, which is far more serious, since most non-Presidential subjects of criminal investigations lack the resources necessary to respond to prosecutorial leaks.

This White House has done an effective job in focusing attention on the prosecutorial abuses of *this* independent counsel, including selective leaks, unfair pressure on witnesses and other questionable investigative tactics. It has provided a civic lesson to all Americans about the importance of the Bill of Rights to anyone suspected of crime. But this important lesson will be undercut unless President Clinton and his administration *generalize* their criticism to prosecutorial abuses directed against *other*s. "Due process for me but not for thee" is an inappropriate message for a President to send. Yet this White House, which has been so appropriately vigorous in defense of President Clinton's rights, has been relatively silent about the rights of others faced with comparable prosecutorial abuses.

To the saying that "a conservative is a liberal who has been mugged," my response is: "Yes, and a Civil Libertarian is a President with an Independent Counsel out to get him." President Clinton has become a civil libertarian, but only when it comes to his own prosecutorial victimization. He is right to complain. Kenneth Starr has employed improper prosecutorial tactics against him, and as President he is neither above nor below the law. But nor is he the only victim of the prosecutorial abuses about which the White House is complaining.

President Clinton's political advisers have told him that supporting the constitutional rights of persons charged with crime is bad politics, and Clinton has listened to their advice. Now he wonders why the American public is not as critical of Starr's tactics as he thinks they ought to be. Perhaps the answer lies in his failure to use his office as a bully pulpit for the constitutional rights of all citizens. It is not too late for the President to begin.

The Secret Service Privilege: Yes and No
July 1998

Should the Secret Service have a privilege to refuse to disclose information it learned in the course of protecting the President or others? That is the question now pending before the courts and soon to be considered by Congress. But the question is being asked too broadly, and both sides—Kenneth Starr's supporters and the President's—are advocating extreme positions. The question should be broken down into various component parts, and the answer should be different depending on the nature of the information being sought from the Secret Service.

There are easy cases at each end of the continuum. Of course the Secret Service should be required to disclose the commission of serious crimes committed in its presence by the President or anyone else. Secret Service officials are law enforcement personnel whose job it is to prevent and disclose serious crimes. Almost no one disagrees with this principle. Equally uncontroversial is the argument that the Secret Service should not be required to disclose its highly confidential methods and techniques for protecting the President. For example, the Secret Service employs undercover agents to infiltrate organizations which pose a threat to the President. It should not be required to disclose the names of these agents nor the organizations that they may have infiltrated. The courts have already recognized a judicially created privilege for undercover agents. Another judicially created privilege should also be recognized. By law, the Secret Service must be present at certain times and places. If an agent, in the course of performing his or her statutory duty, overhears a conversation *already covered by another privilege*, he or she should not be required to disclose that communication. For example, if a Secret Service agent was riding in the President's limousine on the way back from the Paula Jones deposition and overheard the President discussing entirely proper legal strategy with his lawyer, that conversation should be privileged. Normally, if a lawyer-client conversation is overheard by a non-lawyer who was not part of the defense team, the person overhearing the conversation can be compelled to disclose it. There should be a judicially recognized privilege precluding Secret Service agents from disclosing otherwise privileged information, including lawyer-client conversations, national security, executive privilege, spousal privilege, medical privilege and priest-penitent privilege.

Now for the tough cases. What if a Secret Service agent observes the President doing something that is not nice but is perfectly legal, such as having sex with a woman to whom he is not married, or cursing, or being nasty to a subordinate? Under current law, a Secret Service agent is entirely free to write a tell-all book about everything he saw while serving in the White House. Indeed, several who worked for President Kennedy told the writer Seymour Hirsch about alleged indiscretions committed by John Fitzgerald Kennedy. History of course has its claims, and so does privacy. It is appropriate for

Congress to strike a proper balance between these claims, in legislating a calibrated privilege. According to Seymour Hirsch, Secret Service agents not only observed President Kennedy's private sexual encounters, but—along with other presidential aides—may also have facilitated them. Here the question is not so much one of privilege, but rather of the scope of the Secret Service's role. If Congress does not want the Secret Service to facilitate a President's private sexual activities, it should explicitly restrict the role of the Secret Service. But would that be realistic? Imagine an unmarried President, who is dating. Would the Secret Service be "facilitating" the President's sexual activities if they permitted one of the President's dates to share his bedroom? This of course is not a hypothetical, since the jurisdiction of the Secret Service extends beyond our almost-always-married Presidents to several unmarried protectees, including the children of Presidents, former Presidents and presidential candidates. Would the Secret Service be facilitating immorality if it were to permit dates to stay overnight with a protected person?

These are the kinds of questions that Congress does not want to have to address. They are best left to the discretion of the Secret Service. But there is a slippery slope between the Secret Service facilitating alleged adultery by a President and sexual encounters between an unmarried protectee and his or her date.

It is precisely because these questions are so much a matter of degree and do not involve clear points of principle—except at the extremes—that the core issue of whether or not the Secret Service should have a privilege is properly left to the legislative rather than the judicial branch. Having said that, it is also perfectly appropriate for the Justice Department to press its claims in the courts, especially since Kenneth Starr is taking so extreme a view by seeking the testimony of a Secret Service agent who seems to have less to say about what the President may have done than about what he discussed with his lawyer.

The President's Most Important Decision
July 1998

Monica Lewinsky's immunity deal and President Clinton's decision to testify change the nature of the conflict between Kenneth Starr and the President, and raise the stakes for both.

Now that Monica Lewinsky has been given transactional immunity, she is no longer the target of Kenneth Starr's grand jury. The remaining target is President Bill Clinton. We are now therefore confronted with the great constitutional question of whether a sitting President can be indicted by a grand jury and tried by a petit jury in a criminal court, or whether the only recourse is impeachment by the House and trial by the Senate.

The reason this question has now become so important is that the *only* proper function for a grand jury is to gather and consider evidence leading toward a criminal indictment or refusal to indict. It is absolutely improper for an independent counsel or any other prosecutor to use the grand jury process—subpoenas, interrogations outside the presence of counsel, and sworn testimony—in order to obtain evidence to turn over to Congress for purposes of considering impeachment. The separation of power requires that Congress must use its own processes for obtaining evidence leading to impeachment. Congress may not use the courts or the grand jury for this purpose; nor may the court and grand jury be used by an independent counsel for this purpose. Even if Congress could constitutionally authorize the use of a grand jury to gather evidence for impeachment, it has not explicitly done so.

For these reasons, therefore, I expected the President to challenge the subpoena he recently received from Starr's grand jury on the ground that he is not properly the target of a grand jury proceeding, since a sitting President cannot be indicted. This challenge would have forced Kenneth Starr to state his position on whether the President can be indicted, a position that thus far he has refused to state with any clarity. The stage would thus have been set for a great decision by the United States Supreme Court as to whether a sitting President can be indicted and criminally tried. If the answer to that question is no, then it should follow that the President's grand jury subpoena must be quashed. If the answer to that question is yes, then the President must respond to the subpoena, but he is free to invoke his privilege against self-incrimination as well as other privileges.

Without having the answer to these questions it would be difficult for the President's lawyers to give him sound advice as to how he should proceed in the face of a grand jury subpoena. It seems clear that Monica Lewinsky will now testify that the President committed perjury in his Paula Jones deposition when he denied that he engaged in a sexual relationship with her. According to press reports, the definition of sexual relationship given the President before he testified was inclusive enough to cover the kind of sexual contact that Lewinsky will swear she engaged in with the President. Thus if the President were to repeat his sworn statement, he would find himself in a swearing contest with Monica Lewinsky. Nor could the President be sure whether Lewinsky may have some corroboration of her testimony such as the alleged dress—unless of course the President was telling the absolute truth at his Paula Jones deposition. But even if he did testify truthfully, his lawyers should not put him into a swearing contest before a grand jury. It is one thing to be accused of stretching the truth about a marginally relevant fact in a deposition in a civil case that has been dismissed. It is quite another thing to be accused of committing perjury in front of a grand jury.

It is surprising, therefore, that the President has agreed to testify—even on videotape and in the presence of his lawyer. His testimony promises to be the single most important act in his presidency. He must tell the truth, whatever the truth may be. If he did engage in some sexual contact with Lewinsky— and the presumption of innocence requires us to presume he did not—he should admit it. If he did not, then he should deny it. But in either event, his *legal* position will be far worse after he testifies. That is why I continue to be surprised by his decision to increase his legal exposure by testifying before the grand jury. Perhaps he is again accepting the advice of his political advisers over his legal advisers. A source close to the President's lawyers told Geraldo Rivera that it was the President who insisted on testifying in the Paula Jones case, rather than defaulting or settling that case and thereby avoiding the first perjury trap. Now a second—and far more important— perjury trap has been set for the President. He should not make the same mistake twice.

Clinton's Worst Decision: Will It Be Repeated?
August 1998

It should now be apparent to everyone that the single most disastrous legal blunder of the Clinton presidency was the decision to have the President give a deposition in the Paula Jones case and answer questions about his sex life. It is the President's answers in that deposition that endanger his presidency. I have long been arguing that the Jones case should have been settled or even defaulted rather than allowing the President to respond to such degrading and intrusive questions about Gennifer Flowers, Kathleen Willey, and Monica Lewinsky. Had the President settled or defaulted the Jones case, he would have suffered a few days of bad press, but there would be no Monica Lewinsky case, no possibility of a perjury charge, no grand jury testimony and no continuing investigation. Kenneth Starr would be teaching at Pepperdine, and Monica Lewinsky would never have been heard of. But instead, we are talking about semen-stained dresses, perjury traps and possible impeachment.

You would think that the lawyers who advised President Clinton to testify would by now understand how foolish and destructive that decision was. But instead they continue to brag that they "won" the Paula Jones case by getting it dismissed. They refuse to see the forest of possible impeachment for the tree of victory in a civil case. They also continue to criticize those who advocated settlement or default rather than litigation and deposition. If these are the lawyers the President is now listening to, he is in deep trouble.

On a recent Geraldo Rivera show, the host discussed a call he had gotten from a source close to the President's lawyers, presumably in the Paula Jones case. This is how Rivera described it:

> Alan Dershowitz . . . was extremely critical of all the President's lawyers for not settling the Paula Jones case early. It was, as you know, the President's deposition in the now-dismissed lawsuit that led to the discovery of Monica Lewinsky and this current crisis at the White House. One White House source that I will describe as a close ally of the President's attorneys called me today to admonish Professor Dershowitz, first of all, for practicing 20/20 hindsight.

The source also went on to say that it was the President and the First Lady who decided "they had to fight" rather than settle in order to avoid a flurry of new lawsuits.

Whoever made the decision, it was dead wrong. Nor is it wrong only in hindsight. It should have been obvious to any lawyer *before* President Clinton testified. On the Geraldo Rivera show on May 27, 1997—half a year before President Clinton swore that he did not have a sexual relationship with Monica Lewinsky—I outlined the reasons why he could have settled or defaulted the Jones case rather than testify about his sex life.

If the President is still listening to those lawyers who

advised him—permitted him—to walk into a possible perjury trap in the Paula Jones deposition, then he continues to be ill-advised. Whatever the truth may be about the President's relationship with Monica Lewinsky, he should never have testified about it under oath. If he repeats the same mistake twice—if he once again listens to the lawyers who led him into the first possible perjury trap—he will have no one to blame but himself.

What Is Clinton Thinking?
August 1998

President Clinton is about to make the biggest decision of his presidency—perhaps of his life. And it is about whether to tell a "sex lie." It is remarkable that the biggest decision of a presidency is about something so inconsequential on the scale of world problems. It is even more remarkable that on the eve of this momentous decision, the President has probably still not decided which road he is going to take.

President Clinton is a master of assessing options and coming up with the "right" choice—at least in the short run. In this case, he has three basic options. The first is to stick to his story and continue to maintain that he never had sexual relations with Monica Lewinsky. Whether or not this is true, it is in direct conflict with what Lewinsky has sworn to the grand jury. It is also in conflict with what she told Linda Tripp, her mother and her friends. Moreover, the Independent Counsel apparently has physical evidence that is more consistent with Lewinsky's account of a personal relationship than with the President's previous testimony at the Paula Jones deposition which suggested an entirely professional relationship. This evidence includes recorded phone messages from the President, a warmly signed photograph and several gifts.

Then there is the blue cocktail dress. If the dress contains the President's semen, he will have no choice but to change his story. The problem for the President is that he may not know the results of forensic tests when he testifies. This should cause him no concern *if* he had no sexual contact with Lewinsky. He would then *know* that the results will come back negative, at least as to him. But if he did have sexual contact with her, then he may not know whether there is suf-ficient semen for a DNA match. If he knows that he may have left semen on her dress but does not know the results of the test, he will have to act on the assumption that it may be pos-itive. To complicate matters even further, just because *we* don't know the results before he testifies, this does not neces-sarily mean that *he* doesn't know the results. Presidents have a way of learning even the deepest of secrets.

If the President learns—or has to assume—that the test is positive, then his options are reduced to two. The first is that he can refuse to answer incriminating questions about his sex life. He has that right under the Fifth Amendment to the United States Constitution, which provides that no one can be compelled to give testimony that is self-incriminating. He could also invoke other constitutional and statutory objec-tions which would have to work their way through the courts. But he has told the world that he would testify on August 17. He probably made this questionable decision before he knew about the dress, but he can hardly change his mind now on the ground that the dress has surfaced. Perhaps he will come up with other arguments, but they would seem lame in light of his promise to testify. This would leave the President with only one viable option: to change his earlier testimony and statements in which he denied a sexual relationship with Lewinsky. Were he to accept this option, he would probably do it in three stages. First, he would file a detailed affidavit correcting his testimony in the Paula Jones case.[3] Then he would apologize to the world on TV. Finally, and anticlimactically, he would testify before the grand jury. A variation on this option would be to make a deal with the Independent Counsel in which he generally acknowledges his relationship with Lewinsky in exchange for not having to testify as to its details.

If the past is any guide, President Clinton may surprise everyone by coming up with an option no one has considered. The one thing he will not do is listen to the advice of the lawyers who got him into this mess in the first place, by allowing him to be deposed in the Paula Jones case about his sex life. That was the dumbest decision of his presidency, especially since it could easily have been avoided by settling or defaulting that civil suit and simply paying the money. President Clinton was cautioned against testifying about his sex life and urged to settle or default the Jones case. President Clinton and his lawyer ignored that recommendation and provided the testimony that is now the primary basis for Kenneth Starr's continuing investigation. Had he *not* given that testimony in the Paula Jones case, the Independent Counsel would have completed his job without finding any arguable criminal conduct by the President. Still, there is nothing the President has done *so far* that will get him impeached— because it all occurred in the context of a civil suit that has been dismissed. But if he were *now* to deny any sexual involvement with Lewinsky during his grand jury testimony, and if that testimony were to be proved false, he might well lose his presidency.

President Clinton has a difficult decision to make. He should learn from his past mistake and not listen to those who are advising him to repeat the testimony he gave at the Paula Jones deposition.

What if Clinton Were a CEO or a Teacher?
August 1998

Now that President Clinton has acknowledged an inappropriate relationship with a White House intern, the following
argument is being made by pundits, talk show hosts and ordinary Americans: if the CEO of a major corporation had
engaged in an inappropriate relationship with an employee or
an intern, he would surely be fired. If a teacher engaged in an
inappropriate relationship with a student, she would surely
be fired. So why should the President be different? He too
should be "fired"—that is, impeached—for engaging in
what, in a business or academic setting, might well constitute
sexual harassment. On the surface this sounds like a compelling argument. After all, the President is not above the law
and should not be treated more favorably than a CEO or a
teacher. But the argument is specious, for two reasons.

First, what the President has admitted is not sexual harassment under the law. There was no quid pro quo—no promises
or threats in exchange for the sex. And there was no hostile
environment. It is true that many corporations and universities
have policies against even the most consensual sex between
supervisors and subordinates, but those policies go well
beyond the requirement of the law.

Even more important, CEOs and teachers are not elected

by the American people. They are not part of our constitutional system of checks and balances. The United States Constitution provides explicitly that a President may be removed from office only by impeachment, and that impeachment and removal may be based only on "high crimes or misdemeanors." Whatever else it may be, consensual sex with an adult intern does not qualify as a high crime or misdemeanor. It is not even a low crime. It is not a crime at all. It may be wrong, but it is not against the law.

When then majority leader of the House, Gerald Ford, tried to impeach Justice William O. Douglas—who had done nothing more serious than marrying several younger women—Ford claimed that "an impeachable offense is whatever a majority of the House of Representatives considers [it] to be." He was wrong, as he himself recognized when Congress was considering impeaching Richard Nixon.[4] High crimes and misdemeanors must be given their historical meaning. At a minimum, a President must be guilty of criminal conduct. I believe that the criminal conduct must also relate to matters of the state and not to private conduct, unless it is an extremely serious crime like murder. Consensual sex does not qualify. Nor, in my view, does a sex lie told during a deposition in a civil case that was dismissed. Even an attempted cover-up in the civil case—and there is no proof that any such occurred—should not qualify. Committing perjury, obstruction of justice or subornation of perjury in a criminal investigation begins to approach what the framers had in mind.

Richard Nixon's offenses fit within the core definition of high crimes and misdemeanors. They involved a criminal cover-up of matters of state, such as a burglary and break-in directed against political enemies. If "Filegate" had involved criminal activity by the President, that might well qualify for impeachment. But apparently the Independent Counsel has come up dry on "Filegate" and all other matters of state.

Nor should Congress look to the impeachment of judges for precedent regarding the President. Although the Constitution provides the same criteria for impeachment of judges as of the President, judges are appointed to hold their office "during good behavior," which suggest a different interpretation of the criteria for removal. The President is elected for a term of office, and his "behavior" should be judged by the electorate.

Well, then what about Senators and Congressmen who have been thrown out for conduct that might not have been high crimes or misdemeanors? They too are different from the President, for at least two reasons.

First, the Constitution provides a mechanism for their removal that does not require high crimes or misdemeanors. Second, no single Senator or Congressman comprises the legislative branch of our government, just as no single judge comprises the judicial branch. But the President *is* the executive branch. The Constitution says, "The executive power shall be vested in a President. . ." For one branch of government to remove another branch—to substitute one President for another—should require a far more momentous violation of public duty and trust. It should only occur when there is indisputable evidence of a high crime of state, such as existed in the Nixon case.

The allegations against President Clinton—even if proved

—do not qualify as high crimes of state. To impeach a President on the basis of having an improper sexual relationship and then trying to conceal it would trivialize one of our most important constitutional safeguards: the impeachment of a lawless President, who threatens our liberties.

Evaluating Starr's Report
August 1998

As Congress awaits Kenneth Starr's impending report, it is important to evaluate its legal and factual status. The report will be based largely on grand jury testimony, elicited by one side and not subject to cross-examination or impeachment by the other side. Some of the testimony will come from immunized witnesses or witnesses who feared prosecution. Some testimony will come from admitted liars or those with a history of fabrication. Many of the witnesses were "prepared" by prosecutors before they were questioned in front of the grand jury.

In sum, the entire grand jury process is completely one-sided and not subject to the tests of the adversarial process, especially cross-examination, which has been called the greatest engine for determining truth. For these reasons, the grand jury is not supposed to determine "the truth." It is not designed as a truth-finding mechanism. It is supposed to be a method for deciding whether one side's evidence—unchallenged, unimpeached, uncross-examined—meets the threshold for bringing the case *into* the adversarial process. No one should ever conclude that a grand jury indictment, or a report based on grand jury testimony, is true or even close to true.

That has never been the historic purpose of the grand jury, and it is not its purpose today.

Because grand jury proceedings lack the fundamental protections of the adversarial process—the presence of counsel and a mediating judge, the opportunity to object to evidence as irrelevant or hearsay, the right to challenge or respond to evidence—its proceedings are traditionally kept secret. It would be unfair to release to the public the raw data of grand jury testimony, which is comparable to raw FBI files based on gossip, hearsay and innuendo. There is case law to support the proposition that the only legitimate purpose of the grand jury is to gather one-sided information in order to determine the yes-or-no decision whether to indict or not to indict. That is why grand jury *reports* are generally disfavored by the law. That is why a prosecutor in Connecticut was recently sanctioned for expressing his opinion, on the basis of grand jury information, that Woody Allen was probably guilty even though he was not indicted. That is why in the Chappaquiddick case the Massachusetts courts ruled that the one-sided exparte proceedings should never be made public.[5] That is why it would be a terrible mistake—of law, policy and truth—to attribute any significance whatsoever to Kenneth Starr's report, other than treating it as one side's pleading. It is comparable to a complaint in a civil case or an indictment in a criminal case. Nothing more. It is not evidence. It does not overcome—or even weigh against—the presumption of innocence. That is the traditional instruction to the jury.

Indeed, the entire concept of a report based on grand jury testimony is highly suspect as a matter of constitutional law and basic fairness. The very word "report" connotes an objective assessment of the evidence by a reporter who is not an advocate, and who had invited, received and evaluated all the evidence, information and arguments of every side to the controversy. A report based on exparte, one-sided prosecutorial evidence-gathering is a constitutional bastard. It is entirely illegitimate. It misuses the meaning of report. It violates the core spirit of our adversarial system. And it returns us to the bad old days of—pardon the pun—the Star Chamber.

There is serious constitutional question as to whether it is proper to create and issue a report—which is bound to become public—based largely on grand jury testimony, and entirely on a one-sided evaluation of the evidence. Courts have held that it is improper to disclose testimony that was obtained in the absence of counsel and not subject to cross-examination. Such testimony based on unchallenged questions framed by prosecutors will often produce half-truths or worse. "When did you stop beating your wife?"-type questions can be asked in front of a grand jury without objection. There is no opportunity to clear up ambiguities or to present exculpatory evidence. Irreparable damage can be done to witnesses whose grand jury testimony is wrenched out of context and who have no opportunity to present the whole truth. Accordingly, witnesses who have testified in front of a grand jury might well have the right to go to court and seek to enjoin publication of their testimony, or of characterizations of their testimony, or of conclusions drawn from it.

To be sure, Congress has authorized the Independent Counsel to write and deliver a report. But there are grave constitutional questions as to whether a grand jury can be used by an independent counsel to gather information for purposes of making a report to Congress. The sole legitimate function of the grand jury is to decide whether or not to indict. This grand jury has the power to decide that question alone (as well as issues ancillary to that question). But it should have no power to issue a lengthy factual report that purports to contain truths.

From the time Monica Lewinsky was given full transactional immunity, the obvious target of the grand jury has been President Clinton, though Kenneth Starr seems to acknowledge that President Clinton cannot be indicted while serving as President. Accordingly, Kenneth Starr has misused the grand jury to obtain evidence and testimony for inclusion in a report to Congress that will be made public. The implications of using a grand jury to produce a report that, standing alone, may cause severe legal, political and personal consequences creates an extraordinarily dangerous precedent and threatens to impinge the basic liberties of our adversarial system.

How the President's Problems Could Have Been Avoided
August 1998

The problems facing President Clinton—including even possible impeachment—could all have been avoided if the lawyer who represented the President in the Paula Jones case had settled or defaulted that case instead of subjecting the President to a deposition during which he had to testify under oath about his sex life. In the course of that deposition, President Clinton admitted a single sexual encounter with Gennifer Flowers and denied having sexual relations with Monica Lewinsky. In response to a question from his own lawyer, he also swore that Monica Lewinsky was telling the truth when she swore, in an affidavit, that she had never engaged in sexual relations with him.

The Independent Counsel is now, reportedly, going to recommend that impeachment proceedings be opened against President Clinton on the grounds that he committed perjury during that deposition and that he obstructed justice in relation to his defense of the Jones case. Had the Jones case been settled or defaulted well before the deposition, there could be no claim of perjury or obstruction, and it is unlikely that the President would ever have been put in the position of having to admit that he engaged in an inappropriate relationship with Ms. Lewinsky. Though in public Bennett has boasted about his "winning" the Jones case, in private he has tried to blame the decision to have the President testify at the deposition on the President, the First Lady and their political advisers.

He has argued that it was "they" who insisted on fighting the case for fear that settling would open the floodgates of other claims. But if there were any floodgates, they had already been opened by the very public *offer* to settle the case for a sum in the area of $700,000. Any women considering suing would be more encouraged by that offer than by a default, which would have resulted in a considerably lower judgment. Moreover, the statute of limitations had already passed on claims arising *before* the Clinton Presidency.

I know for a fact that Robert Bennett *never told the President* that he had the option of defaulting the Jones case by refusing—on principle—to be deposed about his sex life. The President learned of that option only *after* he testified. Not only wasn't the President told about the option of defaulting rather than testifying, he was never told how the *threat* of default could have helped secure an acceptable settlement. The following tactic could have been tried: Approach the plaintiffs and tell them that the President has decided that he will not testify. Instead he will make a televised address explaining why he must preserve the dignity of the office and the privacy of his family by defaulting the case and refusing to testify—which he had an absolute right to do without even pleading any privileges. (Defaulting is every citizen's absolute right, and the only sanction is that the judgment in the civil case is entered against him.) The case would then move on to the damage phase, where the likely damages would be considerably less than what was offered in the settlement. Typical damages in cases of this sort are well below $100,000. Having told the plaintiffs that there would be no deposition of the President and no trial, the only options left to them would be settlement or default.

Settlement would be far preferable an option than default to the plaintiffs, since they would collect considerably more money and come away with some statement from the President that could be seen as something of a vindication for Jones. Default, on the other hand, would be accompanied by a statement of complete innocence and an explanation as to why it would be wrong for the President to submit to a deposition that might degrade the presidency and violate his family's privacy. The likelihood is that—presented with only the options of settlement and default—the plaintiffs would have accepted settlement. Bennett apparently never thought of this tactic. He certainly never told the President of its availability.

To be sure, defaulting or settling the Jones case would have resulted in a few days of bad press. But President Clinton has been masterful at countering bad press. In any event, he received some bad press for what he said at the deposition: acknowledging a sexual encounter with Gennifer Flowers, after having previously denied it. But in addition to the bad press—which would have been just about the same had he defaulted or testified—he also walked into a perjury trap that now endangers his presidency. Had he *not* testified at the Jones deposition, the Starr investigation would not have had the Monica Lewinsky matter to investigate. That matter has been the centerpiece of the investigation, and the President's deposition testimony—which he did not have to give—is the alleged smoking gun.

It is argued on Bennett's behalf that the entire matter was not his fault, because he was "blindsided" by the President, who assured him that there was no sexual relationship between him and Monica Lewinsky. But it is the job of a lawyer to be skeptical of his client. Bennett certainly should have considered the possibility that the President was too embarrassed about his encounter with Lewinsky to acknowledge it even to Bennett. Bennett has said that if he had been aware of the relationship, he would have "prepared" his client differently. He should have been aware at least of the *possibility* that his client might be put in the position of having to lie in order to conceal an embarrassing sexual encounter from the public, his wife and even his lawyer. A good lawyer always deals in possibilities and probabilities, and takes action designed to prevent the worst of all possibilities—a criminal charge.

Bennett "won" the battle of the Jones case, but in doing so he endangered the President's position in the war for his political survival. Allowing President Clinton to testify about his sex life in the Jones deposition may have been among the worst legal decisions on record. What is even worse is that now Bennett is trying to avoid responsibility for the decision by blaming it on his client.

Sexual McCarthyism
August 1998

As President Clinton commemorated the thirty-fifth anniversary of Martin Luther King's "I Have a Dream" speech, I was thinking about Dr. King's nightmare. At the height of King's influence as a civil rights leader, J. Edgar Hoover tried to bring him down with a sex scandal. Hoover secured evidence that King had engaged in an adulterous liaison with a white woman, and tried to use his evidence to blackmail King into leaving the civil rights movement or even committing suicide.

Senator Joseph McCarthy, and his aide Roy Cohn, snooped around for evidence of homosexuality among their left-wing opponents and succeeded in blackmailing several gay men into becoming cooperating witnesses. Hoover kept records in his home basement of the sexual indiscretions of politicians whose support he needed.

It is probably only a coincidence that Hoover, McCarthy and Cohn could themselves have been subject to blackmail if the truth about their private lives could be proven. The appetite for probing into the sex lives of opponents probably flows more from cynical opportunism than from perverse voyeurism.

Throughout history, the private lives of public figures have been grist for the back-room mill of palace politics. We should not be surprised, therefore, that Kenneth Starr has finally focused on sex as a way to try to bring down President Clinton. Yes, it is about sex. The nation could never understand the complexities of Whitewater and the other financial transactions that were Starr's original mandate. But we can all understand forbidden sex and the efforts by those who engage in it to keep it private.

Surely those Senators, Congressmen and journalists who are posturing so hypocritically about the President's improprieties know of many of their own colleagues who have lied in divorce proceedings in order to spare their children the embarrassment of learning that Daddy or Mommy was not always faithful. Some of them need only look in the mirror, yet they prattle on. The Frenchman who once observed that "hypocrisy is the homage that vice pays to virtue" could have been talking about contemporary Washington. I wonder how many Congressmen and Senators could honestly participate in an impeachment and removal proceeding that focused on extramarital sex, without worrying about what was inside their own closets. A juror who had a problem similar to the one with which the defendant was charged would be disqualified. Were that criteria applied to Congress, I wonder if there would be a quorum.

Do we not realize that authorizing a prosecutor to probe the sex life of a President is far more hazardous to democracy and liberty than anything alleged against President Clinton? Do we fail to understand its implications for future presidents, for other politicians and for ordinary citizens? Are we blind to the dangers of sharpening this weapon of sexual McCarthyism and leaving it lying around to be picked up by future zealots or tyrants? Do we really want to create a permanent office of sex prosecutor whose job it is to police the private lives of our politicians and report the results publicly? Do we want these sex cops to be empowered to grant immunity to one sex partner so that she or he will have no choice but to provide the most intimate details of the other partner's sexual predilections? Can we tolerate the deliberate leaking of these alleged details designed to embarrass our Head of State?

We are assured by Starr and his minions that it is not really about sex, but rather it is about perjury and obstruction of justice. But that has always been the claim of those who use sex as blackmail. It's never the sex itself—that would be too transparent and controversial. It's always the attempt to keep the sex secret. How often throughout history have we heard variations on the theme of "it's not about sex": it's about "national security"; it's about "character"; it's about "business." It's about everything but sex—that is the claim. But it's always really about sex.

Until fairly recently, gay sex was regarded as immoral and wrong. Not surprisingly, many gay men and women went to great lengths to hide their sexual preferences. Most allowed others to believe they were heterosexual, many lied, more even committed perjury when forced to testify about their sex lives under oath. It is in the nature of forbidden sex that those who engage in it also lie about it. When the sex becomes acceptable—as gay sex has among most Americans—the lies stop. That is why most Americans correctly believe that the Starr Report is about forbidden sex, and the inevitable lying was part and parcel of the forbidden nature of the sex itself, rather than a completely separate sin.

The President did make a serious mistake. No, I'm not talking about what he did in private with Monica Lewinsky. That is primarily a family matter. He should never have testified about his sex life in the Paula Jones deposition. He should have refused—on principle—to allow the presidency to be degraded and his privacy invaded. The result would have been to default on the Jones case. It would have been worth it. He has paid a heavy price for that avoidable mistake, but it should not become an excuse for a sexual inquisition.

The average citizen understands that it's about sex, despite efforts by the politicians and the prosecutor to claim otherwise. This sexual McCarthyism must end, or none of us will have the privacy that Justice Louis Brandeis once called the most important right of all.[6]

Keeping Hoover's Name on FBI Building
Sends Wrong Message
April 1993

As I read Anthony Summers's book on the life of J. Edgar Hoover, I couldn't help think how close we allowed ourselves to come to a dictatorship. Although many of the revelations in *Official and Confidential* were known previously, this compilation of abuses into one volume should send shudders down the spine of every American who cares about democracy and due process of law.

Summers's portrait—even discounting the loosely documented allegations of transvestism and homosexuality—is of a cynical tyrant who blackmailed presidents, drove innocent people to suicide and used the most despicable means to try to destroy his enemies.

But the most interesting and disturbing disclosures are not about the blackmailer but about those who submitted to his blackmail—several Presidents of the United States, ranging from Roosevelt to Nixon.

If information is power, then negative information capable of destroying the most powerful people in the world is a veritable nuclear weapon. Hoover had that weapon, and he knew exactly how to use it to achieve his personal ambitions and to settle personal scores.

Hoover specialized in collecting—and selectively disseminating—sexual information about the private lives of public people. Under the pretext of learning this information to prevent the blackmail of high officials with national security secrets, the director of the Federal Bureau of Investigation used it as a sword for his own blackmail rather than as a shield against the blackmail of our enemies.

Hoover was indeed a master. But his mastery was of public relations and propaganda. He fooled a gullible nation into believing that he and his agents were all that stood between Americanism and totalitarianism.

He sure fooled me. As a twelve-year-old, I took my first trip to Washington as part of a class outing. I only have vague recollections of my visit to Congress, the White House, the Supreme Court and the Smithsonian. But I will never forget my morning at FBI headquarters, where I learned about the dangers of "Godless communism," where I saw the "death mask" of John Dillinger and where I watched agents taking target practice. In the years that followed, I became an FBI groupie, reading *Masters of Deceit* and watching as Hoover's G-men systematically captured the "most wanted" criminals in America.

It was only while in college that I began to learn about the darker side of Hoover's FBI, but even then I could not believe that a high official of our government could be guilty of what radicals were claiming Hoover had done. Then in 1973, I was told—by a former government official whose word I trusted—about Hoover's taping of Martin Luther King. Hoover hated King and set out to destroy him. He put in motion a secret plan calculated to get King to commit suicide.

The plan required the Kennedy Administration to approve the wiretapping of King, so that Hoover could secure hard evidence of King's sexual involvement with white women.

Initially, the Kennedy Administration resisted Hoover's demands, but eventually—after Hoover employed his usual blackmail—they relented. They did not know, of course, precisely what Hoover had in mind, but they had to know that the wiretaps were not being installed "for the protection of Dr. King," as former Attorney General Nicholas Katzenbach once tried to rationalize it, or to protect the "national security" of our country, as others tried to explain.

But they did not suspect the use to which the tapes would be put by Hoover. He had the King sex tapes sent to Dr. King's wife, with an anonymous note suggesting that suicide was "the only thing left for [King] to do."

The King plan did not work, as many of Hoover's hare-brained schemes did not work. But Hoover did apparently succeed in driving actress Jean Seberg to suicide, after leaking a story that she was carrying the child of a "prominent Black Panther."

Whether they succeeded or not, Hoover's dangerous plots created an atmosphere of fear and intimidation throughout the nation. I wrote about the King episode while Hoover was still alive, and subsequently discovered that Hoover began a file on me as a result of my critical article. That was his way of trying to control his critics.

Despite this legacy of tyranny and blackmail, Hoover's name is still honored in Washington. The FBI building is called the J. Edgar Hoover Building. This sends precisely the wrong message to young FBI agents and to the public in general: namely, that extortion, blackmail and outright criminality in law enforcement will be honored and rewarded. It is time to remove Hoover's name from all places of honor, and to recognize him for the dangerous criminal he was.

The Sex Cops Go After Both Sides
September 1998

Now Dan Burton, the Republican congressional leader who called President Clinton a "scumbag," has his own little sex scandal. Apparently, the sixty-year-old Congressman has had some "rough spots" in his thirty-eight-year marriage that he tried to smooth over by sleeping with another woman and fathering a child out of wedlock. So begins the tit-for-tat reprisal for the sexual McCarthyism initiated by Kenneth Starr and his Republican supporters.

I promise you, this is not the end. Now that the sex-genie is out of the bottle, every Congressman and Senator who postures about President Clinton's sex life will have his and her closets looked into by the media. Even members of the media who are wringing their hands over Clinton's infidelity may have their own fidelity checked out.

Dan Burton has already apologized "in advance" for everything that is likely to be reported about his infidelity. "Anything you read in the paper that I should be accountable for, I apologize in advance." Maybe some other law-makers will take this advance apology scam to its logical conclusion: apologize even before they engage in the forbidden sex. After all, the real issue with Clinton is not the sex! Right? It's his refusal to apologize. Just get the apology out of the way early, and no one will care what you do.

Burton's brother and mouthpiece is already crying "witch hunt." He's right. But it's a counter-witch hunt. What's fair for the goose . . . and all of that. Why should anyone be surprised when a Congressman who accuses the President of lack of personal integrity has his own personal integrity examined? When Jesus wisely proclaimed that he who is without sin should throw the first stone, he was not only stating a moral principle but also a prudential one. People in glass houses should heed that principle, and everyone in politics these days lives in a house that is not only breakable but also transparent.

I don't know whether the White House's famous attack team has put the media up to investigating Burton's sex life. The media, especially his hometown newspapers, have enough incentive to probe on their own. But even if the White House is behind it, Burton has no cause to whine (unless, of course, the White House improperly used law enforcement files or personnel, but there is no claim of such abuse). Exposing hypocrisy among one's enemies is a legitimate form of counterattack.

In his defense, Burton points to his apology and his promise not to lie about anything that he was caught doing, but he didn't apologize until he was caught and it was about to be made public. So much for genuine repentance. He also swears he didn't lie or do anything illegal. Let's wait and see whether he has ever said anything—to his wife, to his constituents, to a law enforcement official or under oath—that fails the test of "the truth, the whole truth, and nothing but the truth." In general, people who conduct an extensive secret sex life have to lie to keep it under wraps. "Oh, what a tan-

gled web we weave when first we practice to deceive." I doubt
we have heard the last of the Burton scandal. I know we have
not heard the last of other congressional and senatorial scandals. We are just at the beginning of this new round of Lewin-
sky-inspired sexual McCarthyism. There will be many victims, on both sides of the aisle, unless our elected officials
come to their senses—or are brought to their senses by the
realization that this is a dangerous game that can and will be
played by both sides.

Speaker of the House Newt Gingrich who has had his own
history of domestic discord, seems to understand the potentially suicidal nature of a congressional sex inquiry. He has
cautioned, "It's not about scandals in the gossipy sense. It's
about whether or not the law has been violated and, if so, is it
a pattern of violation or is it a one-time event." But Gingrich is
wrong. It is precisely the "sexual behavior in the gossipy sense"
that drives this inquiry and this story. Gingrich is trying to
package it in legalese—they always do!—but it's really about
sex. And whenever politicians engage in forbidden sex, they
try to cover it up—whether they are Republicans or Democrats
or Presidents or Congressmen.

We will now see a flurry of activity designed to lock congressional closets, but it won't work. Once the media is given
a green light of legitimacy to break down those locks, few
closets will remain secure. Kenneth Starr and his supporters
have given that green light. Now all's fair about love and lust
in the political wars. Let's stop this dangerous form of
McCarthyism before it destroys our political institutions.[7]

Sex and Politics
June 1998

There is a dangerous trend among some judges and legal scholars toward arguing that "sexual" speech deserves a lower level of constitutional protection than "political" speech. They claim that political speech lies at the "core" of the First Amendment, while sexual expression lies at its periphery. The fallacy of this reasoning inheres in the assumption that there is a neat line separating the political from the sexual. This was not true at the time our First Amendment was ratified, and it is certainly not true today.

Our founding fathers—the very fact that they were all men suggests an undeniable correlation between politics and sex—were a raunchy crew that included philanderers, pornographers, adulterers and libertines. The commentary of the day partook of the scatological as well as the erotic. Vicious sexual allegations against King George III were common. The *Boston Gazette* called Governor Hutchinson "a rascal" snatched from the "dunghill." And a Tory writer retorted in kind by calling the *Gazette* "dunghill bred" and "Monday's Dung Barge." Another paper called on its readers to smear the houses of loyalists with "Hillsborough Paint" (a mixture of urine and feces). The *New York Journal* likened Mother England to "an old abandoned prostitute crimsoned o'er with every abominable crime." The penchant for scatological epithets did not end with American independence: a leading post-revolutionary case involved a man who publicly expressed his wish "that a cannon had lodged in the president's posterior."

No wonder the framers insisted on protecting freedom of expression in absolute terms: "Congress shall make no law . . . abridging the freedom of speech, or of the press." There was no exception made for sexual expression. Indeed, one of the first exceptions attempted by Congress to the blanket prohibition against passing any law abridging freedom of speech was directed against political, not sexual, speech when the notorious Alien and Sedition laws were enacted in 1798. The first significant congressional attempts to regulate sexual speech did not occur until the Comstock laws were enacted in 1873, which banned speech relating to politico-sexual issues such as birth control.

From the time of the Greeks, laws censoring pornography and obscenity were used against unpopular political speech containing a sexual or scatological component. Sexual censorship has always been used as a cover for political censorship. For example, when the City of Boston censored the musical *Hair* in the late sixties, it publicly focused on the play's nudity, but in private conversations it acknowledged that the real gripe was with the political and religious message.

If there was ever any doubt about the merger between sex and politics, one need merely look at today's headlines. Presidents Kennedy and Clinton were embroiled in politico-sexual scandals, as were Martin Luther King, Jr., J. Edgar Hoover, Benjamin Netanyahu and François Mitterand. Celebrities such as Pamela Anderson Lee, Michael Jackson, Tonya Harding, Pee Wee Herman and Hugh Grant have had their sex lives become the subjects of lawsuits, videotapes and news reports. Religious leaders have been humbled by their sexual meanderings. Catharine MacKinnon and Andrea Dworkin, the high priestesses of sexual censorship, argue that pornography is political propaganda, thus acknowledging that it is "core" speech even under the test that elevates the political over the pornographic. Sex *is* politics and politics *is* sex, and never the twain shall be parted.

Nor is it possible to distinguish between verbal expression and visual expression when it comes to sexual speech. In our age, when the verbal and the visual have become inseparable in such important media as the Internet, television and film, the visual component of a message enhances the verbal and vice-versa. For example, stories about Paula Jones, Tonya Harding and Pamela Anderson Lee have become much more vivid as a result of the publication of sexually revealing visual images.

It is misguided in the extreme, therefore, to lower the threshold of constitutional protection accorded sexual expression. To do so would inevitably lower the threshold for political expression as well, since the two are inexorably intertwined. It is also misguided to talk about the "core" of the First Amendment, since any such core is likely to change over time and with changes in the nature of the prevalent media and messages. The brilliance of the First Amendment—which is a basic contract of governance with the American people—is precisely that it is a broad document designed for all seasons. It should not be read technically, like a last will and testament—lest it become one. Today the primary medium is visual and the primary message seems to be sexual. If you don't believe that, just ask President Clinton.

Focus on the Testimony and Not on the Speech
August 1998

As the world dissects every word of President Clinton's four-minute public speech, Independent Counsel Kenneth Starr's staff are examining the President's four hours of grand jury testimony. That is where the President's new problems may lie, but I now believe he will overcome them. If the President's public speech is any guide to what he swore behind closed doors, it may be possible to discern his new battle plan: to admit to private sexual indiscretions, which are provable but not impeachable; and to deny obstruction of justice and subornation of perjury, which would be impeachable but are not provable.

It is likely that the President admitted to the grand jury only what external physical evidence would probably have established—namely, a semen-producing inappropriate relationship with Monica Lewinsky. Recall that he said in public that his Paula Jones deposition was "legally accurate." This must mean that he denied touching Monica Lewinsky in a sexual manner. For if he did fondle her, then his sworn denial at the Paula Jones deposition of a sexual relationship could be inconsistent with the definition of the vague term provided at that deposition.

Monica Lewinsky has reportedly sworn that the President did touch her in a sexual manner. Thus, Clinton's grand jury testimony may be in direct conflict with Lewinsky's. But there can be no physical corroboration of Lewinsky's claim that the President fondled her. That is a classic "she said, he said" conflict, and there is certainly evidence of her own words on tape that make her credibility sufficiently questionable that no impeachment will rest on her disputed and uncorroborated testimony.

We are told that the President refused to respond to graphic clinical questions about his sexual encounters. He is probably on shaky legal ground, since the court does not recognize a Fourth Amendment right to privacy in grand jury proceedings. But by refusing to get graphic, the President issued a tough political challenge to Kenneth Starr. He dared him to go in front of a judge and to require the President, who has already admitted in general terms to sexual indiscretion, to provide demeaning X-rated testimony. If Starr demands the President's specificity, the court will probably rule against the President, since it may take some graphic description to determine whether his deposition testimony went over the line from nonresponsiveness to perjurious. But in demanding that the President get down and dirty, Starr will hurt his credibility even further. And perjury is a difficult charge to prove against anybody, especially when questions asked at the Jones deposition were so vague, open-ended and ultimately immaterial.

By continuing to attack Kenneth Starr, the President took a calculated gamble. He knew he would alienate such Starr partisans as Senator Orrin Hatch. But he also knew that he would be playing into America's deep dislike of the runaway prosecutor, who breaks the law by improperly leaking grand jury material.

The President's battle plan will work with the average American, but it will not sit well with Starr, Hatch and others who claim that Starr is not interested in the President's private sex life but rather in the steps he may have taken to cover up his indiscretion. In this respect, Starr scored one important point by the President's testimony and speech. The President, in admitting that he was embarrassed about his inappropriate sexual contact with Lewinsky, has provided the Independent Counsel with a motive for why the President may have engaged in a cover-up. But a motive is not proof of a criminal act. And it is unlikely that Starr will ever be able to come up with the kind of indisputable evidence—like the alleged Presidential semen on the dress in the matter of the previously disputed sexual acts—that would be necessary to impeach a President on obstruction-of-justice grounds. Remember that in the Nixon case, there were tapes. Nixon would not have been forced out of office solely on the disputed word of John Dean or anyone else.

So the President's defense is simple and elegant: he will admit to sex and claim it is private and nonimpeachable. And he has put the Independent Counsel to his proof of any impeachable offenses such as obstruction of justice or subornation of perjury. And since there will never be stains or tapes proving obstruction or subornation, the President may well prevail.

CHAPTER V

The Constitutional Crisis: Impeachment, Resignation, Censure?

For Our System's Sake: Don't Impeach
September 1998

Impeachment and removal of an American President is the closest thing, under our system of government, to a bloodless coup or a nonviolent revolution.

Our Constitution provides for presidential impeachment as an extraordinary measure of last resort against an incumbent who has engaged in the most serious kind of official misfeasance or malfeasance. Unlike parliamentary systems, which can remove a prime minister by a legitimate vote of no confidence, our constitutional system does not permit removal on the basis of general dissatisfaction with the policies, preferences or lifestyle of a President.

The removal of a President is different from the removal of a judge, Senator or Congressman (and certainly of a CEO of a corporation). A single judge or legislator is not an entire branch of government; whereas the President is the executive branch of our government.

For one branch to remove another is to upset the delicate system of checks and balances. It should occur only when the President's actions or inaction are clearly inconsistent with his continued services as our head of state—when his nonremoval would pose a clear and present danger to our body politic. Former President Gerald Ford is often quoted as saying an impeachable offense is anything a majority of Congress says it is. But it is forgotten that he was talking about the impeachment of a Supreme Court Justice. He later acknowledged that the criteria for removing a President are much more restrictive, requiring a high crime of state.

It is against this background that the Ken Starr report must be evaluated. At bottom, Starr charges President Clinton with engaging in an improper—though entirely lawful—sexual relationship, and then trying to keep it secret by lying about it in a civil case, trying to prevent the other side from obtaining evidence of it and using the power of his office to defend himself against his enemies. Virtually everyone who engages in an improper sexual relationship tries to hide it. They lie to their spouses, hide the evidence and concoct cover stories.

Clinton is not the first President—or Senator, Congressman or judge—to have engaged in this pattern of conduct. But he is the first to have a special prosecutor assigned to uncover his sexual deceptions.

Not surprisingly, he was caught, and now he has been publicly humiliated by a prosecutorial account of the details of his sexual activities, which is unprecedented in American public life.

Even if every word of the Starr Report—the multiple hearsay, the uncross-examined opinions, the uncorroborated inferences, the rampant speculation—were true, Starr's accusations would not rise to the level of an impeachable offense for an American President. What Starr accuses the President of doing would not even generally be the basis of a criminal prosecution against an ordinary citizen. Litigants in civil cases are rarely prosecuted for lying or covering up peripheral aspects of their sex lives in civil cases, especially dismissed civil cases.

But even if what the President is accused of doing were to be deemed a crime, it is not the sort of "high" crime or misdemeanor the framers had in mind when they established the criteria for impeachment.

Those who argue that it is not about sex, but rather perjury and obstruction of justice, forget the lessons of history. Whenever sex has been used in an effort to bring down an opponent—whether by J. Edgar Hoover against Martin Luther King, Jr., or Joseph McCarthy against political opponents—the argument has always been made that it was not about sex, but rather "national security," "character" or mendacity. But it has always been about sex, and this case is most assuredly about sex as well. Indeed, the original mandate for the Independent Counsel—to investigate Whitewater and then Filegate and then the Travel Office—has come up empty.

Moreover, it is unlikely that all of what Starr alleges could actually be proved at a fair trial, where the burden would be on him. The hearsay, rumors and uncorroborated recollections relied on by Starr to establish some of the most serious allegations would have difficulty passing the crucible of cross-examination and confrontation.

Some are now arguing that it "would be better for the country" if Clinton were to resign or be removed. That is a shortsighted view. The precedent that would be established by forcing a chief executive out of office for what are essentially sexual sins would damage our delicate system of checks and balances and would create the risk of instability. It would also legitimize a form of sexual McCarthyism that would soon become a cancer in our body politic.

For all of these reasons, it would be wrong—as a matter of high principle—for President Clinton to resign. He should fight impeachment and removal, not only for his sake, but also for the sake of our constitutional system and the continued stability of our government.

Starr Report Poses Dangers to Democracy
September 1998

The Starr Report poses a far greater danger to the American system of governance than anything charged against President Clinton. By publishing a report recounting the alleged graphic details of the President's sexual misconduct, the Independent Counsel has forever changed the rules governing public discourse about elected officials. Prior to this report, no self-respecting news organization would have considered publishing the kind of material Starr decided to include—indeed feature—in his referral. No self-respecting prosecutor would include such material in an indictment or present it at a trial. If he tried, the judge would strike it as gratuitous, prejudicial and irrelevant.

But Kenneth Starr did not submit his report to any judge. He alone made the decision what to publish, and his decision evidences a partisan determination to embarrass the President out of office. Starr's tactic seems to be to render the President incapable of governing by exposing his sex life to public ridicule, thereby encouraging others to argue that precisely because of these disclosures the President no longer has the capacity to govern.

Starr's rationale for changing the rules—for publishing the details of an improper but entirely lawful series of sexual encounters—is that the President, by denying that he had sexual relations with Monica Lewinsky, opened the door to details. But Starr went so far beyond what might be necessary to rebut the President's denials that his rationale emerges as a pretext. Consider for example the following multiple-hearsay statement, which appears near the beginning of the report:

> According to Ms. Lewinsky's friend, Neysa Erbland, President Clinton once confided in Ms. Lewinsky that he was uncertain whether he would remain married after he left the White House. He said in essence, "Who knows what will happen four years from now when I am out of office?" Ms. Lewinsky thought, according to Ms. Erbland, that "maybe she will be his wife."

The public disclosure of such alleged conversations and thoughts is irrelevant as to whether the sexual contact between Lewinsky and the President amounted to "sexual relations" under the definition given at the Paula Jones deposition. Its purpose is to embarrass the President and to drive a wedge between him and his wife. In this respect, it is reminiscent of what J. Edgar Hoover, the late director of the FBI, did to Martin Luther King, Jr. Hoover sent a tape recording to Dr. King's wife containing evidence of an adulterous liaison between Dr. King and a white woman. Hoover's purpose was to drive Dr. King out of the civil rights movement and into divorce or even suicide. The verdict of history has strongly condemned this and similar tactics employed by the late Senator Joseph McCarthy, who extorted cooperation from former

Communists by threatening to expose their private sex lives. But the Starr investigation and report threatens to legitimate Sexual McCarthyism as a tactic to embarrass political opponents and drive them out of office.

Consider as well the discussion of "phone sex." By definition, phone sex does not involve any touching and is thus irrelevant to whether the President lied. The same is true of the so-called "cigar" incident, which has become a staple of television comedians and radio talk shows. Yet it too is largely irrelevant to the Jones definition, since it did not involve any direct touching by the President. Even if a prosecutor were to regard these incidents as marginally relevant, anyone with an ounce of judgment and balance would conclude that their enormous prejudicial impact outweighs any minimal probity.

The great danger posed by the Starr Report, in addition to its legitimization of sex as a political weapon, is that it seems designed to take the removal decision out of the hands of Congress and place it directly into the hands of the Independent Counsel. Its purpose is not so much to *begin* a congressional inquiry as it is to embarrass the President and *force* him into resigning because of the details included in the report. If the President were now to resign as a result of these disclosures, our system of checks and balances would be forever damaged. One unelected prosecutor, not even subject to the normal checks under which other prosecutors operate, should not be empowered to bring down a President on the basis of uncross-examined and one-sided accounts of sexual misbehavior and alleged efforts to cover it up.

If President Clinton were to be driven out of office by the

Starr Report, the long-term damage to our system of governance would be incalculable. President Clinton has a duty to resist the dangerous tactic attempted by Starr, to remain in office and to fight vigorously against any attempt to impeach and remove him on the grounds charged in the Starr Report.

Half-Truths About What Is Impeachable
September 1998

In the ongoing debate about what constitutes an impeachable offense, two historical half-truths are being widely circulated. The first is that former President Gerald Ford once said that "an impeachable offense is whatever a majority of the House of Representatives considers to be at a given moment in history." That is true, but he was speaking only about impeaching a judge—specifically, Justice William O. Douglas. The part of his statement that is relevant to the current situation is rarely mentioned. Ford went on to say that to remove a duly elected President "in midterm . . . would indeed require crimes of the magnitude of treason and bribery."

The other half-truth relates to the precedential effect of the proceedings against President Nixon, which led to his resignation in 1974. It is argued that what was *included* in the Articles of Impeachment voted by the House Judiciary Committee—specifically, the "abuse of authority" charge—demonstrates that what the Starr Report alleges constitutes impeachable offenses. What is not mentioned is that the *most* analogous charge was one that was *voted down* by the Judiciary Committee in the Nixon case.

The fourth article of impeachment charged that Nixon had committed tax fraud when he "knowingly failed to report

certain income and claimed deductions . . . which were not
authorized by law." Nixon allegedly failed to pay over
$400,000 in taxes, and knowingly filed a false return, which
is analogous to perjury since it requires signing a false statement under oath.

The issues debated during the House Judiciary Committee hearings are directly relevant to the current debate. Listen
to Democratic Representative Jerome Waldie from California:

> I speak against this article because of my theory that the
> impeachment process is a process designed to redefine Pres-
> idential powers in cases where there has been enormous
> abuse of those powers and then to limit the powers as a con-
> cluding result of the impeachment process. And though I
> find the conduct of the President [Nixon] in these instances
> to have been shabby, to have been unacceptable, and to
> have been disgraceful even, I do not find a Presidential
> power that has been so grossly abused that it deserves rede-
> finition and limiting.

Like Nixon, President Clinton may have engaged in
"shabby," "unacceptable" and even "disgraceful" conduct.
But like Nixon's tax fraud, Clinton's misconduct was more
personal than governmental and did not constitute a gross
abuse of Presidential power.

A key similarity between the two investigations is the non-
governmental nature of the alleged offenses. During the Nixon
hearings, members expressed concern about this issue, arguing "that there is a serious question as to whether something
involving [Nixon's] personal tax liability has anything to do

with his conduct of the office of the President." Democratic Representative Joshua Eilberg from Pennsylvania (who voted for the article) attacked Nixon because the offense was personal, arguing that Nixon's alleged tax fraud was "a clear case of the President of the United States using the power and prestige of his office to enrich himself to the point of grandeur."

Republican Representative Wiley Mayne of Iowa picked up on the personal nature of the conduct in question. He asserted that "the President has a very high obligation to set a good example to the American people in carrying out his personal as well as his public responsibilities." Mayne even rejected Nixon's legal side-stepping—a tactic of which Clinton has been accused—when he argued that "Even if [Nixon's actions] were technically legal, I think it was highly questionable for him to claim such huge deductions for his personal papers." However, despite these strict standards, Mayne still argued against impeachment, protesting the type of intrusive investigation into the President's private life that was used, and has been revisited in the Starr Referral:

> [W]e are here, ladies and gentleman, to determine whether the President should be impeached, not to comb through every minute detail of his personal taxes for the past 6 years, raking up every possible minutia which could prejudice the President on national television.
>
> I certainly do not believe that Madison and the Framers of the Constitution had in mind any such recital as we are hearing here tonight. They did not want the President to be removable simply because he did not enjoy the support and confidence of a majority in the Congress.

The Judiciary Committee, in a bipartisan vote, rejected the personal misconduct charges and limited impeachable offenses to governmental misconduct.

If it is improper to comb through minute details of a President's financial life, how much more improper it is to comb through the details of his sex life and his understandable, though improper, attempts to keep it private.

The full Ford quotation and the full history of the Nixon impeachment articles oppose rather than support any attempt to impeach or remove President Clinton for lying about improper sexual contacts.

Internet Decency and the Starr Report
September 1998

If the Internet Decency Act had not been struck down by the Supreme Court, the Starr Report could not have been sent over the Internet, and many chat-room discussions concerning this important government document might now be illegal. If a national magazine were to come out with a special edition of the Starr Report, it is possible that the new censorship board established under the Military Honor and Decency Act would deem it to be lascivious and therefore unsalable at army PXs around the world. Even the President's taped grand jury testimony—which was shown during the day, when many children were at home for the Jewish New Year— might well violate FCC and network guidelines.

I make these points to illustrate the utter absurdity of trying to distinguish between politics and sex under our First Amendment. Pursuant to the new sexual McCarthyism undertaken by Kenneth Starr, sex is politics and politics is sex. This has of course long been the case even before Starr, but Starr has once again legitimated one of the oldest forms of sexual assault politics. One need only hark back to the bad old days of J. Edgar Hoover, Joseph McCarthy and Roy Cohn to remember how intertwined sex and politics have been.

Now Kenneth Starr has issued a report designed to embarrass President Clinton into resigning. He included descriptions of telephone sex, cigar sex and other forms of erotic interaction that were not relevant to whether the President committed perjury under the definition of "sexual relations" used in the Jones case. The Independent Counsel used the pretext of corruption—the promise of jobs for silence—to investigate the sex life of the President. By showing us the Emperor without clothing, he sought to make it impossible for Clinton to govern.

When the media began to open the closets of Clinton's political enemies—Congresspeople Henry Hyde, Dan Burton and Helen Chenoweth—the Republicans cried foul and called in the FBI. What better organization to go after bad guys who use sex as a political weapon against their enemies than the one that works out of a building named after J. Edgar Hoover—the man who made a career of sexual blackmail!

We live in a nation where sexual hypocrisy reigns. And wherever there is sexual hypocrisy, there will be sexual politics, and its extreme form—sexual McCarthyism. There are two appropriate responses to this form of gutter politics. The first is for American politicians to stop running on their sexual virtues. Our office seekers generally campaign with their adoring spouses, leaving church, Bible in hand, and sexual virtue on the sleeve. That's not the case in most other countries, where the private lives of politicians remain private. When François Mitterand's mistress attended his funeral with their child, there were few raised eyebrows, because Mitterand never pretended to be a paragon of sexual virtue. But when politicians do pretend, it is appropriate to expose their hypocrisy. The other response is to be less embarrassed about sexual disclosures. Congressman Barney Frank acknowledged he is gay and went on with his career.

We are entering an era of reassessment regarding the relationship between sex and politics. Let's talk about it openly and honestly.

Republican Hypocrisy on Perjury
September 1998

A favorite argument being made by some Republicans these days is that unless President Clinton were to be impeached, we would be sending a dangerous message that perjury is acceptable. That message was already sent by Republican President George Bush in the aftermath of the Iran-Contra scandal.

Many of the very Republicans who are now making this slippery argument were resoundingly silent when President George Bush cynically pardoned his former Secretary of Defense Caspar Weinberger for—you guessed it—perjury! Did President Bush's pardon send a message that perjury is acceptable? If not, why not? And if no, why didn't we hear from the same loud claque that is now demanding Clinton's hide?

It cannot be argued that there was any factual doubt about Weinberger's perjury. Weinberger's own secret diary notes proved beyond any doubt that he lied when he denied knowledge of details of Iran arms sales. He had been indicted and was awaiting a trial at which a jury would have determined the facts. It was a slam-dunk case for conviction. But President Bush took the case away from the jury and issued a preemptive pardon. No presumption of innocence shrouds Weinberger, because he forfeited his right to trial by seeking and accepting a politically motivated pardon. Just as an indicted defendant who flees before trial cannot claim any presumption of innocence (unless he returns for trial), so too a pardoned indictee must be presumed guilty, especially when the evidence is as clear as it was in the Weinberger case.

Some Republicans did speak up about the pardon of an indicted perjurer. They applauded it, as Senator Dole did, calling it an act of "courage and compassion." Others agreed. No Republicans feared it would trivialize or legitimate perjury.

Predictably, some Democrats—such as House Majority Leader Richard Gephardt—argued that the pardon constituted a "Presidential approval of violations of the law" and sent a message that lying to Congress was not a serious offense.

Partisan bickering reached its depth when Senator Dole demanded that President Clinton promise not to pardon anyone convicted in the Whitewater scandal, after he was the foremost advocate of the Bush pardons. (Bush pardoned not only Weinberger, but also five others who were convicted of lying to Congress about Iran-Contra.) Former Independent Counsel Lawrence Walsh called Dole's demand "hypocrisy."

The argument made on behalf of Weinberger by his Republican friends—and indeed by President Bush in his pardon statement—was that the Independent Counsel in that case was trying to "criminalize policy differences." The implication was that Weinberger's perjury was only a hook on which to hang a political prosecution. The fact that he lied under oath was deemed trivial by those who agreed with his policies. I guess that for them perjury as a means toward a politically desirable result is perfectly all right. They did indeed trivialize perjury, when committed by their friend,

even on an issue of circumventing the constitutional authority of Congress. But these same Republicans now wring their
hands about a sex lie designed to cover up something far less
significant than what Weinberger's lie concealed.

The lesson of the Bush-Weinberger pardon is that there is
a selective morality in Washington even about perjury. Republican perjury is different from Democratic perjury, just as
Republican sex seems to be different from Democratic sex.
Many of those who argue that perjury is perjury, that it doesn't
matter whether it is about sex, seem to limit their passions to
their political opponents and develop amnesia about their
friends.

Despite being indicted and pardoned for perjury, Weinberger remains an honored figure within the Republican Party
and in business and academic circles. The fact that he lied
under oath is viewed by some as "patriotic." Others see it as
business as usual in Washington. Lying, like sex, serves as an
excuse to go after one's political enemies and to support one's
cronies. No wonder most Americans believe that the current
crisis is neither about sex nor lying. It is about politics—dirty,
partisan politics. An election should not be undone on the
basis of such selective moralizing.

Had Clinton Listened to His Lawyers
September 1998

Lawyers have been getting a bad rap in the Starr-Clinton controversy. Conventional wisdom appears to be that Clinton got himself into trouble by following the advice of his lawyers and ignoring the advice of his political advisers. Nothing could be further from the truth. If Clinton had followed the advice of his lawyers, he never would have testified about his sex life in general or his relationship with Monica Lewinsky in particular. I am certain that Robert Bennett advised him to settle the Jones case (my criticism of Bennett is that he never told the President about his option of defaulting the Jones case). I am also certain that David Kendall advised the President not to testify in front of the Starr grand jury, but instead to invoke his legal rights, including his constitutional right not to be subpoenaed by a grand jury seeking evidence for impeachment. It is likely as well that the President's lawyers were against his finger-shaking public denial that he had sexual relations with "that woman."

In each of these cases, where legal strategy required silence, political expediency mandated speaking. And speaking about an impermissible sexual affair almost always means lying. Lawyers understand that remaining silent is always better than risking a lie. It is politicians—looking to tonight's television news, tomorrow's headlines and the day after tomorrow's poll—who often advise risky speech over cautious silence. The problem with this White House is that it always thinks in short-term tactics rather than long-term strategy. It is willing to risk next month's legal disaster to avoid today's political annoyance.

Now it is being argued that the time has come to stop listening to the lawyers, with their hair-splitting distinctions, and start listening to the politicians. Impeachment, we are assured, is a *political* not a legal proceeding. That is dangerous advice. If Clinton were to acknowledge that impeachment is a political proceeding, he would invite self-serving political decisions by election-hungry Congressmen and Senators. Impeachment is neither strictly legal nor strictly political. It is constitutional. It is an act that goes to the essence of our structure of government. It should be decided neither on hair-splitting legal distinctions nor on self-serving political expediency. It is a high act of state. And should be decided on the basis of whether the President has engaged in the kind of constitutionally mandated misconduct which warrants the extraordinary remedy of undoing a quadrennial election.

President Clinton should raise the level of the debate from the legal-political to the constitutional. He should talk about the structural issues of checks and balances and his duty to resist unconstitutional efforts by the legislative branch to usurp his Presidential powers. He should focus attention away from the sordid details of the Starr Report and onto the elevated principles of the Constitution. He should remind our citizenry that ours is not a parliamentary system, where a head of state serves at the pleasure of the legislature and may be removed by a parliamentary vote of no confidence. The President is elected directly by the people at specified intervals. The President and his party pay a political price for his personal indiscretions, but unless they rise to the level of impeachable offense, he must serve out his term.

Nor may he simply resign to serve the political interests of his party. He has a duty to complete his term, unless he has committed an impeachable offense. It would not be in the long-term interests of our nation's stability for President Clinton to be forced out of office by the Starr Report. A resignation by Clinton would legitimate Starr's sexual McCarthyism and encourage future efforts to try to overthrow presidencies by investigating into the lives of our Presidents.

Clinton should stop listening to day-to-day politicians who become blinded to history by looking at too many polls. He should begin listening to constitutional lawyers, historians and men and women of deeper and longer vision. He should look back at the history of the mistakes that led him to where he is today, and heed the words of the philosopher who warned that whoever neglects the errors of history is doomed to repeat them. The errors of this presidency are of political shortsightedness, which caused legal mistakes, which, in turn, have created a constitutional crisis.

Carts, Horses and Impeachable Offenses
September 1998

The decision by Republican lawmakers to conduct evidentiary hearings on what the President may have done *before* holding legal hearings on what constitutes an impeachable offense puts the factual cart before the constitutional horse. In any fair system, the law must come before the facts. Until we know what the constitutional criteria are for impeachment, evidentiary hearings must necessarily become fishing expeditions.

Levrenti Beria, the notorious former head of the KGB—the Soviet version of our own J. Edgar Hoover—once said, "Give me the man and I will find the crime." There is the danger that Republican partisans will define impeachable offenses after the fact to tailor fit whatever the factual investigation may uncover, instead of first defining the offense and then conducting objective hearings to determine whether President Clinton did or did not commit any such offense.

If it is true that consensual sexual activity—an affair followed by an attempt to cover it up—is not the sort of "high" crime contemplated as impeachable by our Constitution, then it is gratuitous, unfair and degrading to conduct extensive hearings into whether President Clinton did or did not touch specified portions of Monica Lewinsky's anatomy. Only if Congress—or at least the judiciary committee—were *first* to vote that sex lies are impeachable should an evidentiary hearing on the issue *follow*. But the Republicans are afraid to debate and vote on the criteria first, because they know that the people have made up their minds that sex lies should not be deemed impeachable.[1] They are hoping therefore, that a wide-ranging fishing expedition may turn up *something* impeachable. That is why they want to expand the inquiry beyond Monica Lewinsky and into issues such as Whitewater, Filegate and the Travel Office—despite Starr's failure to refer these issues to Congress in his report.

Moreover, the Republican leadership seems unwilling to define in advance what the procedures should be in any inquiry. This is like the kid who wants to start the game without rules and then decide on the rules only after he has established his position. Rules must come first if they are not to become after-the-fact justifications for ad-hoc unfairness.

One reason why the Republicans think they can get away with these un-American approaches to justice is that the road to impeachment is uncharted. The Constitution provides few guideposts. It does specify that the Chief Justice shall preside at the removal trial of a president, but it does not specify his role. Does he merely keep decorum, or does he also rule on evidentiary questions, and if so, are his rulings final or are they subject to appeal to the entire Senate? Can the Chief Justice decide whether the evidence must prove the offense beyond a reasonable doubt or by the lower standard of preponderance, and, if so, whether the evidence meets the appropriate standard? Can the Chief Justice, or the Senate, disqualify a Senator from participating if he or she has a clear conflict of interest? Does the Chief Justice "instruct" the Senate on the law, as a presiding judge instructs a jury, and, if so, how does he decide what the "law" of impeachment is? These are important questions that have never been definitively resolved. They require extensive research, analysis and debate.

One case does not a precedent make, and there has only been one removal trial of an American president, and that trial was conducted by a kangaroo court rife with regional and ideological division. It is not a model that should be followed blindly. In that case, it took an act of great courage by an individual Senator to avoid a constitutional disaster that might well have been followed by bloodshed. As recounted by John F. Kennedy in his book *Profiles in Courage*, a young Republican Senator named Edmund Ross sacrificed his political career by casting the deciding vote against removal. This is how Senator Ross explained his unpopular vote:

> In a large sense, the independence of the executive office as a coordinate branch of the government was on trial. If the President must step down...upon insufficient proofs and from partisan considerations, the office of President would be degraded, cease to be a coordinate branch of the government, and ever after subordinated to the legislative will. It would practically have revolutionized our splendid political fabric into a partisan Congressional autocracy... This government had never faced so insidious a danger... If Andrew Johnson were acquitted by a nonpartisan vote...America would pass the danger point of partisan rule and that intolerance which so often characterizes the sway of great majorities and makes them dangerous.

This is a time for courage, not politics as usual. Our nation needs Congressmen and Senators with vision beyond today's partisan advantage, media headlines and public opinion polls. We must begin with a great debate about constitutional principles, not a tawdry recounting of degrading details.

Can This End with a Deal?
October 1998

As Congress moves toward impeachment hearings, the possibility of a deal—a global resolution of the entire investigation of President Clinton—is being considered. It will not be easy.

In order to be global, a deal would require the agreement of the President, Congress, the Independent Counsel, and perhaps Judge Susan Webber Wright, who presided at the Paula Jones case. A separate deal with Paula Jones herself seems likely, if long overdue.

Congress cannot compel Kenneth Starr to agree not to prosecute Clinton after he leaves the presidency, but it is unlikely that Starr would want to be perceived as a deal breaker, if there was a widespread consensus in favor of resolution. But if he believes that Congress is being too soft on the President, Starr might balk. Perhaps the deal could be sweetened for Starr by having Judge Norma Holloway Johnson drop her pending investigation of grand jury leaks by the Independent Counsel's office.

Nor could Congress make Judge Wright promise not to sanction Clinton for his misleading answers in the Jones deposition, but if the President resolves his case with Jones, it is less likely that Judge Wright would feel the need to proceed with any contempt citation.

An even more serious problem is that the most likely sanctions that would be imposed by Congress as part of a settlement raise serious constitutional questions. Our Constitution specifies the checks and balances that each branch of government may impose on the others. Impeachment is one such check. There is nothing about "censure." Of course no one could stop Congress from censuring the President, just as no one could stop the President from censuring Congress. (The Supreme Court could not censure either of the other branches, because it is expressly limited to deciding cases and controversies.) But it is unclear what the effect of a congressional censure would be.

The only President ever to be censured was the feisty Andrew Jackson who refused to accept the Senate's censure. He sent the following message to the Senate:

> The Executive is a coordinate and independent branch of the Government equally with the Senate; and I have yet to learn under what Constitutional authority that branch of the Legislature has a right to require of me an account . . .

Three years later, when Jackson's party won back control of the Senate, the censure was "expunged." Senator Robert C. Byrd, who has written a history of the Senate, believes that censure of a President "lacks a constitutional basis."[2]

An intriguing variation on censure has been proposed by Professor Jonathan Turley of George Washington University

Law School: impeach the President but don't remove him. That would send a powerful message of disapproval akin to sanction, but well within the constitutional authority of Congress. I respectfully disagree. Impeachment—like indictment—should never be used to send a message. It is a prelude to removal and should be used only to put a President on trial for an impeachable offense. Using it any other way "lacks a Constitutional basis."

So does imposing a monetary fine on a President. It has been suggested that the President be punished by being made to pay for the cost of Starr's investigation or by having his pension reduced or by being fined for his misconduct. But the prohibition on Bills of Attainder and ex post facto punishment would prevent Congress from singling out the President for after-the-fact punitive sanctions. At least that is what the law says. But if all parties agree to a deal—even an unconditional deal—who will object? It is in the nature of deals that they are sometimes extra-legal. I have pleaded clients guilty to nonexistent crimes as part of a plea bargain—with the approval of the judge. I have seen unconstitutional conditions—agreeing to attend church, to give blood and to join the army—agreed to as part of a deal. If an unconstitutional tree falls in a forest and no one complains, has the law really been violated? We may never know, if the major players in the Presidential investigation all agree to the terms of a deal.

There will certainly be some constitutional purists in Congress who will refuse to violate their oath of office—which requires them to abide by the Constitution. They might even seek the assistance of the judicial branch, but I think the courts would be reluctant to interfere in what would be seen as a political compromise in the national interest.

So, after all is said and done, this constitutional crisis, which began with an unseemly sex act in the Oval Office, may end with an unconstitutional compromise.[3]

Chronology of Events Leading Up To the Clinton/Starr Constitutional Crisis[4]

1976   Bill Clinton is elected Arkansas Attorney General.

1978   Arkansas Attorney General Bill Clinton and Hillary Clinton join with James B. and Susan McDougal to borrow $203,000 to buy 220 acres of land in Arkansas's Ozark Mountains. They soon form the Whitewater Development Corp., intending to build vacation homes.

Clinton is elected governor.

1980   Clinton loses his reelection bid and enters private legal practice.

James McDougal, who served briefly as Governor Clinton's economic development director, quits government to buy a small bank in Kingston, Arkansas. He loans $30,000 to Hillary Clinton to build a model house on a Whitewater lot.

1982 McDougal buys a small savings and loan, and names it Madison Guaranty.

Clinton is again elected governor.

1984 Federal regulators begin to question the financial stability and lending practices of Madison Guaranty, criticizing Madison's speculative land deals, insider-lending and hefty commissions paid to the McDougals and others.

Clinton is reelected governor.

1985 James McDougal holds a fund-raising event at Madison Guaranty to help pay off a $50,000 Clinton campaign debt. Investigators later determine some of the money was improperly withdrawn from depositor funds.

McDougal hires the Rose Law Firm, where Hillary Clinton is a partner, to do legal work for the ailing savings and loan.

Hillary Clinton and another Rose lawyer seek state regulatory approval for a recapitalization plan for Madison.

1986 McDougal borrows $300,000 from a company owned by David Hale, a former Little Rock judge. Hale's company receives federal funds from the Small Business Administration to lend to disadvantaged business owners, but an investigation ten years later alleges that he lent up to $3 million to political figures instead.

Citing improper practices, federal regulators remove McDougal as Madison Guaranty's president, but he retains ownership.

1988 As part of a general housekeeping of old files at the Rose Law firm, many of the Madison land contract files are destroyed.

Hillary Clinton writes James McDougal to ask for power of attorney to sell off remaining Whitewater lots and clear up bank obligations.

1989 Madison Guaranty collapses. The federal government shuts it down and spends $60 million bailing it out.

James McDougal is indicted on federal fraud charges related to his management of a Madison real estate subsidiary.

1990 McDougal is acquitted.

1992 The Clinton presidential campaign gathers information on Whitewater and Madison Guaranty. A report commissioned by the campaign claims the Clintons lost $68,000 on Whitewater, an estimate later adjusted down to somewhat over $40,000.

The Federal Resolution Trust Corp., investigating causes of Madison's failure, sends a referral to the Justice Department that names the Clintons as "possible beneficiaries" of illegal activities at Madison.

January 1993   Clinton's first term as President begins.

May 1993   White House fires seven employees in the Travel Office, possibly to make room for Clinton friends. An FBI investigation of the office ensues, allegedly opened under pressure from the White House to justify the firings.

June 1993   Deputy White House Counsel Vincent Foster files three years of delinquent Whitewater corporate tax returns.

July 1993   Foster is found dead in a Washington area park. Police rule the death a suicide. Federal investigators are not allowed access to Foster's office immediately after the discovery, but White House aides enter Foster's office shortly after his death, giving rise to speculation that files may have been removed from his office.

Fall 1993   RTC's criminal referral is sent to Paula Casey, U.S. attorney in Little Rock. Casey—who was Clinton's former law student, volunteered on his 1992 campaign, and was appointed by Clinton—recuses herself.

November 1993   The Clintons hire David Kendall as their personal attorney.

December 1993   The White House agrees to turn over Whitewater documents to the Justice Department, which had been preparing to subpoena them. These documents include files found in Foster's office.

January 12, 1994 President Clinton asks Attorney General Janet Reno to appoint a special counsel to investigate his involvement in the Whitewater real estate venture and its relationship to Madison Guaranty, a failed Arkansas savings and loan.

January 19, 1994 Because the independent counsel law had lapsed, Reno uses her own authority to name Robert B. Fiske, Jr., a former Federal prosecutor.

January 1994 Fiske announces he will also explore a potential link between Foster's suicide and his intimate knowledge of the developing Whitewater scandal.

February 1994 Republican attorney Jay Stephens is appointed to head the Resolution Trust Corp.'s investigation of the failure of Madison Guaranty.

March 1994 Webster L. Hubbell abruptly resigns as associate attorney general after allegations are raised about his conduct at the Rose Law Firm. Two of Clinton's top political advisers call business friends and line up more than $500,000 for Hubbell, including $100,000 from the Lippo Group. Hubbell is later convicted of fraud and serves eighteen months in jail.

May 3, 1994 Clinton hires lawyer Robert S. Bennett to handle the sexual harassment lawsuit brought against Clinton by Paula Corbin Jones.

Summer 1994   The House and Senate Banking committees begin hearings on Whitewater.

August 5, 1994   A U.S. Court of Appeals panel refuses to reappoint Fiske as special counsel, citing a possible conflict of interest because he was appointed by Clinton's attorney general, Janet Reno. Kenneth W. Starr, a former federal appeals court judge and U.S. solicitor who worked in the Reagan and Bush administrations, succeeds Fiske as the Independent Counsel to investigate Whitewater-Madison matters. He reissues subpoenas for documents, such as the Rose billing records of Hillary Clinton.

January 3, 1995   The Democratic majority on the Senate Banking Committee releases a report finding that no laws were broken in the Whitewater matter.

April 22, 1995   Starr interviews the Clintons privately.

June 1995   Monica Lewinsky begins working at the White House

July 18, 1995   The Senate Special Whitewater Committee, chaired by Republican Alfonse D'Amato, begins hearings on Whitewater and on Foster's suicide. D'Amato is also a chairman of Republican Bob Dole's presidential campaign. The hearings last eleven months.

August 17, 1995   A grand jury charges James and Susan McDougal and Arkansas Governor Jim Guy Tucker with bank fraud relating to questionable loans.

October 26, 1995 The Senate Whitewater committee issues forty-nine subpoenas to federal agencies and others involved in the affair.

December 12, 1995 White House associate counsel William H. Kennedy III, who worked at the Rose Law Firm, refuses to release subpoenaed notes of a 1993 meeting between administration officials and the President's lawyers about Whitewater.

December 20, 1995 The Senate votes along party lines to enforce the subpoena. The next day, the White House drops its claim to attorney-client privilege and releases the notes. They prove vague and do not reveal any illegality, but contain the phrase "Vacuum Rose law files WWDC Docs—subpoena."

January 4, 1996 Hillary Clinton's billing records from the Rose Law Firm are found on a table in the White House residence book room after two years. Clinton aide Carolyn Huber says she found the bills in August 1995 but didn't realize their significance until coming across them again. The documents include copies of bills for Hillary Clinton's legal work, showing she performed sixty hours of legal work for Madison in 1985 and 1986.

January 8, 1996 In a commentary titled "Blizzard of Lies," *New York Times* columnist William Safire describes Hillary Clinton as "a congenital liar." White House Press Secretary Michael McCurry said if Clinton were not President he "would have delivered a more forceful response to that [column] on the bridge of Mr. Safire's nose."

January 22, 1996   Kenneth Starr subpoenas Hillary Clinton in a criminal probe to determine if records were intentionally withheld, the first time a wife of a sitting president has been subpoenaed.

January 26, 1996   Hillary Clinton testifies before a grand jury about the discovery and content of the billing records.

March 4, 1996   Whitewater trial of Arkansas Governor Jim Guy Tucker and the McDougals begins in Little Rock.

April 17, 1996   Monica Lewinsky leaves the White House for public affairs post at the Pentagon.

David Hale, the former owner of a government-funded lending company who has pleaded guilty to two felonies, testifies at Whitewater trial that in early 1985 then governor Bill Clinton pressured him to make a fraudulent $300,000 loan to Susan McDougal and asked that his name be kept off the transaction.

April 28, 1996   Clinton testifies on videotape as a defense witness for just over four hours. He denies Hale's charge. The tape is played to the Whitewater trial jury on May 9.

May 28, 1996   Governor Tucker and the McDougals are convicted of nearly all the fraud and conspiracy charges Starr lodged against them ten months earlier.

June 1996   The White House acknowledges that during four months in late 1993 it wrongly collected FBI background reports on hundreds, including prominent Republicans. Director of personnel security Craig Livingstone later takes responsibility.

June 17, 1996 "Second" Whitewater trial begins. Arkansas bankers Herby Branscum Jr. and Robert Hill are accused of illegally using bank funds to reimburse themselves for political contributions, including contributions to Clinton's gubernatorial and presidential campaigns.

June 18, 1996 The Senate Whitewater committee finishes its investigation. Republicans and Democrats remain divided in their respective reports on whether the Clintons committed any ethical breaches.

July 7, 1996 President Clinton testifies on tape for the second Whitewater trial.

July 15, 1996 Jim Guy Tucker resigns as governor of Arkansas.

July 16-17, 1996 Deputy White House Counsel Bruce Lindsey, named an unindicted co-conspirator in the Branscum-Hill trial, testifies about his role as the treasurer of Clinton's gubernatorial reelection effort in 1990. He says he never sought to conceal from regulators two large cash withdrawals he ordered.

July 18, 1996 President Clinton's videotaped testimony from July 7 is aired at the trial. In it, Clinton denies naming the two defendants to unsalaried state posts in exchange for contributions to his 1990 gubernatorial campaign.

August 1, 1996   In a major setback for Starr's investigation, Branscum and Hill are cleared on four counts of bank fraud by a federal jury, which deadlocks on seven other charges.

August 19, 1996   Former governor Tucker receives a suspended four-year sentence after his doctor testifies that he would likely die of liver disease if imprisoned. Tucker is placed under home detention and fined $319,000.

August 20, 1996   Susan McDougal is sentenced to two years in prison for her role in obtaining an illegal loan for the Whitewater venture.

September 4, 1996   Susan McDougal, who had considered cooperating with prosecutors, refuses to answer questions. She enters jail for contempt of court rather than testify in front of a grand jury.

September 23, 1996   An FDIC inspector general's report concludes Hillary Clinton drafted a real estate document that Madison Guaranty Savings & Loan used to "deceive" federal regulators in 1986.

November 1996   Clinton's former campaign strategist for the 1992 election, James Carville, announces plans to attack Starr as a partisan hatchet man with a right-wing agenda.

February 17, 1997 Starr announces he will leave his post as independent counsel in August to become the dean of Pepperdine University Law School in California. After much criticism, Starr reverses his decision four days later and resolves to keep his post until after the investigation is completed.

April 10, 1997 On a radio talk show, Hillary Clinton denies that hush money was arranged for former law partner Webster L. Hubbell. She says Whitewater reminds her "of some people's obsession with UFOs and the Hale-Bopp comet some days."

April 14, 1997 James B. McDougal is sentenced to three years in prison for his conviction on eighteen fraud and conspiracy charges. Starr requested a reduced sentence for McDougal for assisting the prosecution.

April 22, 1997 The U.S. District Court extends the Whitewater grand jury's term six more months, until November 7, after Starr says he has "extensive evidence" of possible obstruction of justice.

April 25, 1997 8th U.S. Circuit Court of Appeals, overruling a lower court, says the White House must turn over subpoenaed notes to Starr. The notes, for which the White House claimed attorney-client privilege, were taken by White House lawyers when investigators questioned the First Lady.

May 2, 1997 The White House announces that it will appeal the decision on the subpoenaed notes to the Supreme Court.

June 23, 1997   The Supreme Court refuses to hear the appeal, and the White House turns over the notes.

June 25, 1997   The *Washington Post* reports that Whitewater prosecutors have been questioning Arkansas state troopers about President Clinton's personal life, including possible extramarital affairs he may have had while Arkansas governor.

July 15, 1997   Starr's office concludes that Vincent Foster's death in 1993 was a suicide.

July 30, 1997   Susan McDougal, imprisoned for contempt of court, is moved into a federal detention facility after seven months in two Los Angeles jails, much of which she spent locked in a windowless cell twenty-three hours a day. The move comes a week after the American Civil Liberties Union filed a lawsuit alleging that McDougal was being held, at Starr's request, in "barbaric" conditions in an attempt to coerce her to testify.

December 26, 1997   Lewinsky leaves the Pentagon.

January 7, 1998   In an affidavit in the Paula Corbin Jones sexual misconduct case, Monica Lewinsky denies that she had a sexual relationship with Clinton.

January 12, 1998   Tripp tells prosecutors in Starr's office that she has a tape on which Lewinsky says Clinton's confidante Vernon E. Jordan, Jr., encouraged her to deny having an affair.

January 13, 1998 Tripp wears a hidden microphone for the FBI and records a conversation with Lewinsky, during which Lewinsky is said to have described her conversations about her affidavit with Jordan.

January 15, 1998 Starr's office tells the Justice Department about Tripp's accusations. A panel of federal judges authorizes Starr to investigate whether Clinton and Jordan encouraged Lewinsky to lie under oath in her affidavit.

January 16, 1998 Attorney General Janet Reno, in consultation with the federal appeals court that oversees independent counsels, approves an expansion of Starr's probe.

January 17, 1998 President Clinton, testifying under oath to lawyers in the Paula Jones sexual harassment case, denies having had sexual relations with Lewinsky. He acknowledges having had an affair with Gennifer Flowers, a charge he previously denied.

January 21, 1998 News accounts first appear of the alleged affair between the President and Ms. Lewinsky.

January 22, 1998 At a photo session with Palestinian leader Yassar Arafat, President Clinton responds to questions about his alleged sexual affair with Lewisnky, saying "... the allegations are false, and I would never ask anybody to do anything other than tell the truth." Vernon Jordan comes before the cameras, acknowledging he helped arrange job interviews for Lewinsky but denying he told her to lie about an affair with the President.

January 26, 1998   During a televised White House news conference, Clinton states, "I did not have sexual relations with that woman... I never told anybody to lie."

January 27, 1998   Hillary Clinton, appearing on NBC's "Today" show, says the Lewinsky controversy has been fabricated by a "vast right-wing conspiracy." In a seventy-two-minute State of the Union address, President Clinton makes no mention of the Lewinsky controversy.

January 29, 1998   After inconclusive discussions between Lewinsky's lawyer, William H. Ginsburg, and Starr's prosecutors, negotiations on an immunity deal protecting Lewinsky from prosecution for perjury appear stalled.

January 30, 1998   Linda Tripp breaks her silence, faxing news organizations the scoop that she overheard a 2 a.m. Lewinsky-Clinton phone call. U.S. District Judge Susan Webber Wright rules the Secret Service can disregard subpoenas related to presidential affairs.

February 10–11, 1998   Lewinsky's mother, Marcia Lewis, testifies for more than six hours over two days and leaves the Federal District Court in Washington looking physically shaken and emotionally distraught.

February 11, 1998   Contradicting the President's sworn testimony, retired Secret Service agent Lewis Fox tells the *Washington Post* that he saw Lewinsky and Clinton together alone in the Oval Office in late 1995.

February 22, 1998 The White House asserts executive privilege to restrict Bruce Lindsey's testimony.

March 3, 1998 Clinton friend Vernon Jordan testifies before Starr's grand jury.

March 5, 1998 Jordan testifies for a second day before Starr's grand jury. Ginsburg argues before a Federal district judge in Washington that Starr's office had made, then retracted, a firm offer of immunity for Lewinsky in return for her full testimony. Starr denies making such a deal.

March 8, 1998 James McDougal dies just months before he hoped to be released from prison.

March 15, 1998 Former Clinton aide Kathleen Willey appears on CBS's "60 Minutes," and says the President made unwelcome sexual advances towards her in a room adjacent to the Oval Office at the end of 1993. "I just remember thinking, 'What in the world is he doing?'" she said.

March 16, 1998 Responding to Kathleen Willey's claims, President Clinton tells reporters, "Nothing improper happened." Meanwhile, the White House releases friendly letters Willey wrote to the President after he allegedly made unwelcome sexual advances.

March 20, 1998 The President's lawyers file court papers responding to Jones's 700 page filing. Attorney Bob Bennett tells reporters the report does not contain information on Jones's sexual past.

March 21, 1998   Clinton invokes executive privilege in an effort to limit grand jury questioning of aides Bruce Lindsey and Sidney Blumenthal.

April 1, 1998   Judge Wright dismisses Jones's sexual harassment suit against the President, saying Jones' complaint, even if true, would not constitute a violation of law.

April 16, 1998   Paula Jones announces she will appeal the dismissal of her case. Starr says there is no end in sight to his investigation, and officially declines the Pepperdine job, which was being held open for him.

April 23, 1998   Susan McDougal, refuses yet again to testify before Starr's Little Rock grand jury.

April 25, 1998   Starr and deputies question Hillary Rodham Clinton about Whitewater for nearly five hours at the White House. The testimony is videotaped for the Little Rock grand jury.

April 29, 1998   A Federal district judge rules that Lewinsky did not have an agreement with the Independent Counsel that would give her immunity from testifying.

April 30, 1998   Starr's grand jury indicts Webster Hubbell and his wife on charges of tax evasion.

May 4, 1998   Susan McDougal is indicted by Starr's Little Rock, Ark., grand jury on charges of criminal contempt and obstruction of justice.

May 5, 1998   In Washington, U.S. District Judge Norma Holloway Johnson denies the White House executive privilege claim.

May 11, 1998   The Lewinsky family hires Judy Smith, a veteran media relations specialist.

May 22, 1998   Johnson rules that the Secret Service must testify in the Lewinsky case, finding there is no legal basis for a privilege shielding agents from testifying about the President.

May 28, 1998   In a Los Angeles F.B.I. office, Lewinsky gives handwriting, fingerprint and voice samples.

June 2, 1998   Lewinsky dismisses Ginsburg and hires Jacob A. Stein and Plato Cacheris. One week later, the new lawyers discuss possible immunity for Lewinsky with independent counsel prosecutors.

June 4, 1998   The Supreme Court denies Starr's request that it bypass lower courts to expedite rulings on the Secret Service's claim of privilege and the White House claim that government attorneys are covered by the attorney-client privilege.

June 13, 1998   In an article in *Brill's Content*, editor Steven Brill accuses Ken Starr of illegally leaking information about the Lewinsky case to reporters. Starr responds immediately, denying the charge.

June 25, 1998   Susan McDougal, suffering from a severe spinal condition, is released from prison after a judge commutes her sentence to time served.

June 30, 1998   Linda Tripp testifies before Starr's grand jury.

July 1, 1998   A federal judge dismisses tax charges against Clinton friend Webster Hubbell brought by the Independent Counsel.

July 7, 1998   A three-member federal appeals court rules unanimously that there is no privilege protecting the Secret Service from testifying before Starr's grand jury.

July 17, 1998   After Supreme Court Chief Justice William Rehnquist refuses to block the order on Secret Service testimony, the agents report to the grand jury. Prosecutors issue a historic subpoena ordering Clinton's testimony.

July 27, 1998   A federal appeals court rules that Lindsey's testimony is not shielded by attorney-client privilege. Lewinsky talks with prosecutors.

July 28, 1998   Lawyers for Lewinsky broker an immunity deal with Starr in which she promises "full and truthful testimony" in exchange for a sweeping grant of immunity from Federal prosecutors. Her mother, Marcia Lewis, is also given immunity.

July 29, 1998   Clinton agrees to testify by videotape from the White House, and prosecutors withdraw their subpoena. Legal sources say Lewinsky has given prosecutors a dress that she says may contain evidence of a sexual encounter with the President.

August 3, 1998   The President surrenders a DNA sample to Starr for comparison with a reported semen stain on a dress owned by Monica Lewinsky.

August 4, 1998   Chief Justice William Rehnquist rejects the White House's appeal that Bruce Lindsey and other White House lawyers should be covered by attorney-client privilege.

August 6, 1998   Monica Lewinsky begins testifying before Kenneth Starr's grand jury in Washington, D.C.

August 7, 1998   Chief U.S. District Judge Norma Holloway Johnson orders a probe into allegations that Kenneth Starr's office has leaked information to the press about testimony to the Lewinsky grand jury.

August 17, 1998   President Clinton testifies to the Lewinsky grand jury via closed circuit television from the White House's Map Room. That evening, he makes a televised address to the nation about his testimony and admits that he had a "not appropriate" relationship with Ms. Lewinsky, but insists that he never told anyone to lie about it.

August 20, 1998   The former White House intern returns to testify before the grand jury as Starr attempts to pinpoint suspected inconsistencies with the President's testimony.

August 23, 1998   House Speaker Newt Gingrich says that Starr would have to provide proof of "a pattern of felonies" for Congress to launch an impeachment inquiry.

August 25, 1998   House Minority Leader Richard Gephardt calls the President's behavior "reprehensible."

September 3, 1998   Connecticut Democratic Senator Joseph Lieberman calls Clinton's behavior "disgraceful" and "immoral."

September 4, 1998   During a press conference in Ireland, the President says, "I made a big mistake. It is indefensible and I am sorry."

September 9, 1998   Starr sends to Congress his report of possible impeachable offenses by President Clinton. Separately, the President tells a Florida audience, "I let you down. I let my family down. I let this country down. But I'm trying to make it right. I'm determined to never let anything like that happen again."

September 11, 1998   The House of Representatives votes to release the Starr report on the Internet. The White House releases a preliminary rebuttal. At a prayer breakfast, President Clinton says, "I don't think there is a fancy way to say that I have sinned," and for the first time expresses regret publicly for hurting Monica Lewinsky and her family.

September 12, 1998 The White House releases a revised rebuttal to Starr's report.

September 18, 1998 Amidst partisan bickering, the House Judiciary Committee votes to release the videotape of the President's grand jury testimony plus more than 2,800 pages in additional documents.

September 21, 1998 Video recording of Clinton's grand jury testimony is aired around the world.

September 25, 1998 The House Judiciary Panel votes to release thousands of more pages in additional documents, including edited conversations between Lewinsky and Tripp.

Notes

How Did We Get Here?

1. See Maureen Dowd, "Maladroit Du Seigneur," *New York Times*, 30 September, 1998, p. A23. ("He would be laughed out of any locker room in the country.")

2. Prior to the Lewinsky matter becoming public, there were widespread reports that the President limited his extramarital sex to oral gratification since he believed that it did not constitute Biblical adultery and it gave him verbal deniability regarding sexual relations. This history actually strengthens his legal claim that he did not commit perjury when he denied having what he regarded as sexual relations with Lewinsky. A twenty-eight-year-old waitress was quoted by *Newsweek* as saying that as Clinton continues to define sex more and more narrowly, she begins to think of herself as a virgin!

3. Paula Jones's lawyer have recently revealed that the Jones

lawsuit could have been settled at one point for no money with just a simple apology from President Clinton which made it clear that Paula Jones did not do anything wrong in the hotel room.

4. For example, Lawrence E. Walsh, who investigated the Iran-Contra affair, "worried that a long-term consequence of the Lewinsky investigation was 'the burlesquing of law enforcement in this country.'" See Jill Abramson, "Tightening Tensions Signals an Uglier Round," *New York Times*, 19 August 1998, p. 22. James McKay, who investigated Edwin Meese, also has said that the Lewinsky inquiry went too far. He also criticized the salacious detail that Starr included in his report, believing that "'the point could have been made without the specific pornographic discussions.'" See Michael Winerip, "Starr Report Recalls Outlook of a Preacher in Rural Texas," *New York Times*, 13 September 1998, p. 1.

5. "Material" is not easy to define, but it requires the allegedly false statement to be relevant to or probative of the central issues in the case.

6. See Tom Kuntz, "Impeachment or Censure: Either Precedent's Ugly," *New York Times*, 13 September 1998, sec. 4, pg. 5.

7. The allegation closest to the current allegations against President Clinton—that Nixon filed a false tax return—was voted down by the Judiciary committee (see Chapter V). The allegation against Clinton that is closest to those against Nixon is Filegate, which has not (at least to this point) been proven.

8. The impeachment and removal trial of Andrew Johnson took three months. See Kuntz.

Chapter I

1. The Independent Counsel Act was reinstated by Congress in June 1994. See David E. Rosenbaum, "Clinton May Gain as Counsel Bill Clears," *New York Times*, 22 June 1994, p. 1.

2. In order: the Warren Commission investigated the assassina-

tion of President John F. Kennedy, Vice President Spiro Agnew resigned, President Nixon fired Archibald Cox, President Gerald Ford pardoned former President Nixon, and President George Bush pardoned Caspar Weinberger.

3. Webster Hubbell later resigned from his position as Associate Attorney General in March 1994 because of investigations into his billing practices while working at the Rose Law Firm with Hillary Rodham Clinton. He pled guilty to embezzlement in December 1994 and served eighteen months. He was later indicted again on tax-evasion charges in April 1998, but the indictment was dismissed. See Ruth Marcus et. al., "Judge Dismisses Hubbell Tax Case; Starr Exceeded His Authority, Court Rules," *Washington Post*, 2 July 1998, p. A1.

4. The Knesset (the Israeli parliament) passed the law for the direct election of the prime minister in 1992, and Benjamin Netanyahu was the first directly elected prime minister of Israel in 1996. See Shlomo Avineri, "A Well Meant Reform," *Jerusalem Post*, 10 March 1995, p. 5; and Gerald M. Steinberg, "A Flawed Presidency," *Jerusalem Post*, 21 August 1998, p. 9.

Chapter II

1. One of Mikva's first acts as White House Counsel was to assure President Clinton that Starr would be completely fair. Later, after leaving his position as White House Counsel, Mikva changed his mind, calling Starr "the first Grand Inquisitor in American history," and "someone [he could] not vouch for." See Michael Winerip et al., "Ken Starr Would Not Be Denied," *New York Times Magazine*, 6 September 1998, p. 6; and Abner J. Mikva, "Letter to the Editor," *New York Times*, 1 April 1998, p. 22.

2. On June 19, 1998, federal judge Norma Holloway Johnson issued a sealed ruling (the ruling was unsealed on August 7, 1998) that justified an inquiry into the "serious and repetitive" leaks

emerging from Ken Starr's office. This followed the publication of an interview of Starr by Steven Brill in which Starr acknowledged discussing the investigation with reporters: "'I have talked with reporters on background on some occasions.'" Brill reported that he had "personally seen internal memos from inside three news organizations that cite Starr's office as a source" and that "six different people who work at mainstream news organizations [had] told [him] about specific leaks." At the time of this publication, the inquiry is still pending. See Steven Brill, "Pressgate," *Brill's Content*, July/August 1998, pp.123-151; James Bennet, "Judge Cites Possible Breaches of Ethics Guidelines by Starr," *New York Times*, August 8, 1998, p. 1; and "Excerpts from Order Regarding Leaked Grand Jury Information," *New York Times*, August 8, 1998, p. 10.

Chapter III

1. William Safire, in his column "Blizzard of Lies," called Hillary Clinton "a congenital liar." In response, White House Press Secretary Michael McCurry responded that "the President, if he were not the President, would have delivered a more forceful response to that on the bridge of Mr. Safire's nose." See William Safire, "Blizzard of Lies," *New York Times*, 8 January 1996, p. 27; Neil A. Lewis, "White House Says President Would Like to Punch Safire," *New York Times*, 10 January 1996, p. 11.

2. Cardinal Bernardin was the Roman Catholic Archbishop of Chicago when a former seminary student filed a suit against him in 1993 for having abused him seventeen years earlier. Bernardin denied the charges, and the suit was dropped four months later when the accuser no longer trusted his recollections because he had them while with an amateur hypnotist. See Peter Steinfels, "Cardinal Bernardin Dies at 68; Reconciling Voice in Church," *New York Times*, 15 November 1996, p. 1.

Chapter IV

1. On June 2, 1998 William Ginsburg was dismissed by Monica Lewinsky, departing "by mutual agreement" according to Lewinsky's spokesperson Judy Smith. See Franics X. Clines, "Lewinsky Dismisses Her Lawyer and Hires Washington Veterans," *New York Times*, June 3, 1998, p. 1.

2. On July 28, 1998, Lewinsky was granted full immunity by Kenneth Starr in exchange for her cooperation in the investigation of President Clinton. See Don van Natta, "Lewinsky, Given Immunity, Reportedly Agrees to Tell of Pact with Clinton to Lie," *New York Times*, 29 July 1998, p. 1.

3. Neither Clinton nor his lawyer did this, and Judge Wright responded by implying that she might impose sanctions on Clinton. See also Andrew P. Napolitano, "Clinton's Perjury and His Lawyer's Ethics," *Wall Street Journal*, 24 September 1998, p. A18.

4. See "Half-Truths About What Is Impeachable" for a further discussion of the Ford statement.

5. The case involved Senator Edward Kennedy's car accident in 1969 in which his passenger, Mary Jo Kopechne, died.

6. Just as McCarthyism led to political loyalty oaths, so too sexual McCarthyism will inevitably lead to sexual loyalty oaths. Already one Congressional candidate has signed an "integrity" oath that he never had "an extramarital affair" or a "homosexual relationship," and has challenged his opponent to sign the same oath. See William Presecky, "Mueller Signs His Oath of Integrity," *Chicago Tribune*, 24 Sep. 1994, p. 1.

7. Since the writing of this article, two other vocal lawmakers in the Clinton investigation have had their sexual indiscretions revealed. First, Republican Representative Helen Chenoweth of Idaho criticized Clinton for the "sordid spectacle" of his affair and launched a campaign commercial stating that "personal conduct and integrity does matter." On September 10, 1998, Chenoweth

admitted that she had had a long-time affair with a married man: "I was involved in a relationship that I came to regret, that I'm not proud of."

Second, an Internet magazine named *Salon* revealed that Republican Representative Henry Hyde—who is the Chairman of the House Judiciary Committee considering Ken Starr's report and whether or not to initiate impeachment proceedings—had an affair three decades ago with a married woman. Hyde called his actions "youthful indiscretions," though he was in his forties and the affair lasted four years and broke up the woman's family.

Chapter V

1. Senate Majority Leader Trent Lott said that he thought "bad conduct is enough, frankly, for impeachment," to which Maureen Dowd of the *New York Times* responded, "Americans understand perfectly that if good conduct were required in Washington, the city would have closed shop long ago." See Maureen Dowd, "Maladroit Du Seigneur," *New York Times*, 30 September 1998, p. A23.

2. See Tom Kuntz, "Impeachment or Censure: Either Precedent's Ugly," *New York Times*, 13 September 1998, sec. 4, p. 5.

3. Another clue to the intent of the framers can be gleaned from the investigation of Alexander Hamilton's alleged misuse of Treasury Department funds in 1792 and 1793. Hamilton was accused of giving Treasury money to convicted swindler James Reynolds to play the stock market. However, when Hamilton admitted that the money was his own and was given to Reynolds because Hamilton wanted to hush up the affair he had with Reynolds' wife, Congress concluded that Hamilton's misconduct was private and therefore not impeachable. See Robert Fear, "Founding Fathers Are Used to Build a Case for Clinton," *New York Times*, 4 Oct. 1998, p. 37.

4. This chronology is made up in large part from timelines found at the following Internet addresses:

http://www.washingtonpost.com/wp-srv/politics/special/
whitewater/timeline.htm

http://www.nytimes.com/library/politics/081798clinton-
timeline.html

http://cgi.pathfinder.com/time/daily/scandal/timeline.html